HOOP DREAMS

HOOP
DREAMS

BY PAUL ROBERT WALKER

BASED ON THE FILM BY
STEVE JAMES, FREDERICK MARX, & PETER GILBERT

Turner Publishing, Inc.

ATLANTA

Published by Turner Publishing, Inc.
A Subsidiary of Turner Broadcasting System, Inc.
1050 Techwood Drive, N.W.
Atlanta, Georgia 30318

ISBN 1-57036-197-5

Distributed by Andrews and McMeel
A Universal Press Syndicate Company
4900 Main Street
Kansas City, Missouri 64112

First Edition
10 9 8 7 6 5 4 3

Printed in the U.S.A.

• Contents •

• Playground Basketball •

*Right now, I want to play in the NBA. That's something
I dream—think about all the time, playing in the NBA.*
                                        —WILLIAM GATES, age 14

William Gates holds the basketball confidently between
his hands and gazes at the rusted metal hoop, outlined
against the Chicago sky. There is no net and no one
watching—just a boy, a ball, and a hoop.

Pushing the ball to the pavement, William begins to
dribble. One step, two steps, three steps. On the fourth
step he takes off from his left foot, soars through the air,
switching the ball easily from his left hand to his right,
and slams it through the hoop. Wham!

Landing gracefully, he retrieves the ball and dribbles
toward the basket for a lay-up. Then he dribbles to the
top of the key and takes a turn-around jump shot. Swish!
Nothing but net. If there was a net.

William stops for a moment and cradles the ball
loosely under his arm. It's a hot summer evening in
1987. Although it's almost dark, he can clearly see the
huge, looming, orange-brick buildings of Cabrini Green,
a housing project near downtown Chicago. Most of the
families who live in Cabrini Green are black and poor.
Many depend on welfare payments from the state in
order to get by, and those who work have low-paying
jobs. It's a tough neighborhood, where gangs and drug

dealers fight over their turf. But it's home to thousands of honest, hardworking people with talent and dreams. People like William Gates.

William wants to play in the NBA. "That's something I dream about all the time," he says, "playing in the NBA."

That night in 1987, there are hundreds of boys from Cabrini Green who dream of playing in the NBA. And throughout the hot streets of Chicago, there are thousands more. How many will really make it? How many have the right combination of talent, intelligence, and hard work? How many will even get the opportunity to develop their talent?

Although he's only fourteen years old, William already has the strength and self-confidence of an older boy. He's developed his skills by playing with his older brother, Curtis—a star player in high school and junior college. Curtis received a basketball scholarship to a big university, but he didn't get along with the coach and dropped out before graduating. Now Curtis 'no longer dreams of playing in the NBA himself. He dreams for William, and he works with him whenever he can, sharpening the younger boy's moves and pounding him hard beneath the boards.

"I just bang him and bruise him," Curtis explains. "I'm trying to let him know right now you're going to get hit, you're going to get knocked down, you're going to get banged around, so you better get used to it now."

William lives with his mother, Emma, a warm, kind-hearted woman who raised six children after their father deserted the family. Mrs. Gates works as a nurse's assistant at a home for the elderly. It's a low-paying job, but

8

Emma Gates and her family are better off than many families of Cabrini Green. Instead of the huge, looming high-rises where gunmen and drug dealers stalk the hallways, they live in a more pleasant two-story apartment building with a back door that leads straight to the basketball court. Curtis lives with his wife and daughter in the same building, just two doors away.

Mrs. Gates is happy that her sons love basketball, happy they have something that really matters to them. But she insists that they pay attention to school as well. Curtis got his high school diploma, and his graduation photo is proudly displayed in the living room. Mrs. Gates wants William to get his diploma, too—and go on to college if he can. But more than anything, she wants William to stay away from the gangs that control the streets around Cabrini Green.

"My mother, she was like mother and father to me," William says respectfully. "She don't want me really hanging around over here that much because of the gangs."

That summer, William looks forward to attending St. Joseph's High School—a private school west of Chicago, far from the tough streets of Cabrini Green. The tuition and other fees at St. Joseph's are far too much for Mrs. Gates to pay, and normally William would never have an opportunity to attend such an expensive school. But his basketball ability has opened the door.

During William's eighth-grade season, two assistant coaches from St. Joseph's saw him play on his grammar school team. They were so impressed that they told their head coach, Gene Pingatore, "You've got to see this guy." Coach Pingatore is a legend in the world of

Illinois high school basketball. For five of the last six years, he's guided St. Joseph's to the prestigious state tournament held at the University of Illinois in Champaign. One of the secrets of Coach Pingatore's success is finding talented young players like William, who have developed their skills on the inner-city playgrounds.

When Pingatore saw William play, he was just as impressed as his assistants. He invited the eighth grader to attend St. Joseph's the following year and offered him a scholarship that will pay about half of his tuition and fees, based on his financial need. Cabrini Green has an organization called C.Y.C.L.E. that will cover the rest of William's expenses.

Many boys from the tough neighborhoods of Chicago have attended St. Joseph's on scholarship and played for Coach Pingatore, but one very special boy saw all his dreams come true. His name is Isiah Thomas. When he left St. Joseph's he went on to become one of the greatest guards in basketball history, first at Indiana University, then with the Detroit Pistons of the NBA. If it happened for Isiah, maybe it will happen for William.

A few miles west of Cabrini Green, Earl Smith cruises along in his comfortable late-model car. A confident, heavy-set man, Mr. Smith played some serious basketball in his younger days. Now he has a good job as an executive at an insurance company in downtown Chicago, but he still loves the game and he loves helping young people. So on the weekends, Smith serves as an unofficial talent scout for several high schools in the area, combing the parks and playgrounds for players who have the potential for stardom, players who might make a difference to a high school team. One of the schools that he represents is St. Joseph's.

In the summer of 1987, Earl Smith watches a group of young teenagers playing a fast-paced, half-court game on a Chicago playground. All the boys are good players for their age, but Smith notices one boy who's faster than the others. Like William Gates, he is fourteen years old, just graduated from eighth grade. He's skinnier and shorter than William, but he whirls and twirls like a ballet dancer and blows by defenders like they aren't even there.

"He's got the quickest first step I've seen in about five years," Smith tells a companion. "I'll bet you a steak dinner in four years you'll be hearing about him. I don't even know anything about him."

After the game, Mr. Smith introduces himself to the skinny boy with the quick first step. The older man explains who he is and tells the boy about the basketball program at St. Joseph's High School—the school where Isiah Thomas started out on the road to success. He invites the young player to a basketball camp. If the boy does well at the camp, then maybe St. Joseph's would offer him a scholarship to help pay for his education, based on his financial need. Mr. Smith wonders if the boy is interested.

The boy with the quick first step flashes a big smile. His name is Arthur Agee, and he's definitely interested.

• Tryout Camp •

When I get into the NBA, first thing I'm gonna do, I'm gonna see my Momma. I'm gonna buy her a house. Gonna get my Dad a Cadillac Oldsmobile so he can cruise to the games.

—ARTHUR AGEE, age 14

A few days later, Earl Smith pulls up outside the Agee home in a west Chicago neighborhood called Garfield Park. At first glance, it looks very different from the faceless housing projects of Cabrini Green. It's an older neighborhood, with smaller red-brick apartment buildings and two-flats mixed in with stores and vacant lots. Arthur's family lives on the second floor of a two-flat that has a big cement porch leading down to the street.

But although Arthur's neighborhood looks more pleasant than Cabrini Green, it's just as tough and dangerous. Gangs and drug dealers control the streets, and people struggle to pay for food and rent. The Agees are better off than some families in the neighborhood, because both of Arthur's parents work.

His father's name is also Arthur, but most people call him Bo. A handsome, charming man, Mr. Agee works at a food-processing plant—hard work for low wages. He was a basketball star himself until he ran into trouble as a young man. Now he's excited about the possibility of sending Arthur to St. Joseph's, away from the problems of the neighborhood.

"I just want Arthur to have more, you know, have a better life than I had," Mr. Agee explains. "I don't want him experiencing bad things that I went through in life."

Arthur's mother, Sheila, is a pretty, intelligent woman who works as a nurse's assistant for the minimum wage, similar to the job that Mrs. Gates has. She has high hopes for Arthur, too, although she's worried about him going so far away from home every day. Mr. and Mrs. Agee and Arthur's younger brother, Joe, accompany him to the tryout. Arthur's older sister, Tomika, is busy with her own life.

Arthur rides in the front seat of Earl Smith's car while the rest of the family follows in their own car. Along the way, Earl explains to Arthur what's expected of him at the tryout. "Your role today, Arthur, is to impress the coaches. Try not to be too fancy. Take the open shot when you have it. Play good defense and make good passes. The rest of it just play natural."

Arthur nods seriously. He knows all about playing natural. It's his schoolwork that has him worried. "I'm hoping I'm going to St. Joe's and play," he says, "but first I got to get my books straight, and hopefully, come out and impress the coaches."

As the car continues to roll westward into the suburbs, Arthur thinks about the idea of the new school. He admits that it's all a little scary. "I never been to a school way out before, and I would be going to a school with different kids, different races."

Most of the students at St. Joseph's are white. For fourteen years, Arthur Agee has lived in a world of mostly black people. It's natural to feel frightened at a

13

new experience; yet it's interesting, too. It has possibilities. As they draw near the school, Arthur looks out the window at the comfortable houses and perfectly manicured lawns of suburban Westchester. "You can look at the scenery," he says, "and meet new friends."

When Arthur enters the doors of St. Joseph's High School with his family, he immediately notices things he hasn't seen before. "I saw a rug, flowers, clean hallways—things that I didn't see at an ordinary school." For Arthur, an ordinary school is in the inner city of Chicago, a school with too many students and not enough money to pay for everything the students need. Right away, Arthur realizes that St. Joseph's is different.

Before the camp, Arthur and his family meet with head basketball coach Gene Pingatore. As he talks to Arthur and his family, Coach Pingatore leans back comfortably in his chair, cleaning out the bowl of his unlit pipe. His tie hangs loosely to the side, and he speaks with the confident authority of a man who knows exactly what he's doing. He's used to people listening to him; he's talked to scores of families just like the Agees.

But for Arthur and his parents, this is a new experience. Someone is offering them a very special opportunity. Mr. Agee sits upright in his chair; his youngest son, Joe—who they call Sweetie—sits on his lap. He and Mrs. Agee listen very carefully to what this white man from the suburbs is offering their son. Arthur tries to focus on Coach Pingatore and look very serious, but his eyes can't help drifting up to the big color picture of Isiah Thomas on the coach's wall.

"Basketball has to be second to your academics," Pingatore begins. "If you don't get your grades, you're not going to play. If you work hard at your grades and if you work hard at basketball, then I would be able to help you as far as going to college. I can't promise you where you're going to go or if you're going to be a star. But I guarantee that I would help you to get into the school that would be best for you. So I'm making a commitment to you if you make a commitment to being a part of this kind of program."

At the camp, there are about forty young players. Most of them are white boys from the local area. But a few are like Arthur and William—black boys from the inner city whom Coach Pingatore is recruiting to improve his team. William has a slight injury, so he doesn't play much. There's no reason to risk aggravating the injury. Pingatore already knows what William can do, and William has already agreed to attend the school. Arthur is an unknown; this is the first time the St. Joseph's staff has seen him play.

On the court Arthur moves quickly and easily, with the style that made him a stand-out on the playground. He feels confident about his performance. "It was like a million guys trying to be better than the other," he says later. "To me, I was better than all of them."

But Gene Pingatore has seen thousands of good players over the years, and he's not easily impressed. "I can see the playground in him," he explains. "I can see the talent, but I don't see the confidence." Despite his doubts, Coach Pingatore offers Arthur a chance to play at St. Joseph's.

At the end of the camp, Pingatore proudly introduces the most famous graduate of St. Joseph's High School. "High School All-American. All-American from Indiana University. Five-time NBA All-Star. Isiah Thomas."

As the boys watch with big, startled eyes, Isiah Thomas walks out onto the floor of the St. Joseph's gymnasium. He's wearing the blue uniform of the Detroit Pistons, and he flashes his famous smile. Arthur is so excited he can barely keep from shouting. It's Isiah! For real! Right in front of him!

Thomas is a small man, really—not much bigger than some of the boys. But he's the biggest star they've ever seen. And he used to play right on the same floor where they're playing this afternoon. Coach Pingatore has asked his former star to come today, not just to impress the boys, but to teach them something, too.

"Hello," Isiah Thomas begins. "How are you? In everybody's neighborhood, there's a guy who can really play. He can shoot the lights out." Thomas pantomimes a smooth jump shot. "Every time down court—swish, swish, swish.

"Then he goes to St. Joseph's High School and the guy gets cut. And you say, 'Tom was real good. Why did he get cut?' See, Tom didn't learn the fundamentals of team basketball, which is what you're learning how to play."

Arthur listens to every word that Thomas says. "If Isiah says it," Arthur thinks, "then it must be right." And that's just what Coach Pingatore hopes Arthur and the other boys will think, because the biggest difference between being a playground star and a high school star is learning to play for the good of the team.

After he's finished talking, Thomas gives Arthur a different kind of lesson. The five-time NBA All-Star invites Arthur to play him one-on-one. "I know the boy can play," Thomas tells Arthur's father, "so I'm gonna play him hard."

Isiah Thomas starts with the ball at the top of the key. Arthur crouches down to guard him, his heart beating with excitement. Thomas fakes left, right, then left again and blows by Arthur for an easy lay-up. Arthur just smiles and shakes his head. Up in the stands, his parents and Earl Smith are smiling, too. No one really expects Arthur to guard Thomas, but it's a thrill to watch them play together. Just the two of them: Isiah Thomas and Arthur Agee.

While the NBA star signs autographs for the eager boys, Gene Pingatore thinks back to the days when Thomas first came to St. Joseph's. "With Isiah," he remembers, "I just knew he was gonna be a great one. He had the total combination of personality, confidence, talent, intelligence, and you could see that in the kid.

"I think I see it in one kid that's coming here. If you watch him on the basketball floor he flows with a smoothness and confidence and strength that you don't see in every kid. He could become a great player."

The kid Coach Pingatore is talking about—the kid who might be the next Isiah Thomas—is not Arthur Agee. The kid is William Gates.

• Arthur's Freshman Year •

I just never been around a lot of white people. It's a little hard, but I can adjust to it.

—ARTHUR AGEE

It's 5:30 A.M. in the middle of winter, and the snow-covered streets of Chicago are still dark. In the Agee house, the lights are on as Arthur gets ready for school. After eating breakfast, he puts on a hooded sweatshirt over his regular shirt. Then he zips up his heavy, orange parka over the sweatshirt, pulls a green knit cap down to his ears, slips on his fur-lined gloves, and hangs his book bag over his shoulder. Like an arctic explorer, he heads out into the cold, icy streets to begin his long journey to school.

Arthur starts off on a train called the "El," short for "elevated" because the train rattles along above the city streets. When he gets out into the suburbs, he transfers to a bus for another long ride. He has to be very careful to make the connection, because if he misses it he'll be late for school and St. Joseph's has very strict rules about tardiness. Finally, he has to walk the last half mile through the snowy streets of Westchester. The trip takes him an hour and a half each way—so he spends three hours every single day just getting to and from school. It's a long, hard trip, especially in the cold Chicago winter. It's almost the same trip that William

Gates makes from Cabrini Green. And it's the same trip that Isiah Thomas made before them.

Once he arrives at St. Joseph's, Arthur finds himself in a very different world from what he's used to. Most of the students are white, and all of the students are boys. Discipline is strict, with many punishments for breaking the rules. Religion is a required class, something Arthur never experienced in the public school. And all the academic classes are tougher than anything he's ever encountered before. Tests show that Arthur begins his freshman year at St. Joseph's working on a fourth or fifth grade level. He's placed in the lowest group of the general education program.

Discipline is strict in the basketball program, too. In the locker room, another black player shows Arthur a list posted on the bulletin board. "Hey, Arthur," he says. "Hey, man, do you know that if you miss a free throw, they count 'em up and you have to pay fifteen cents for each one you miss? And at the end, if you don't pay it, they gonna make you run fifty laps, and you *still* gotta pay the money."

Arthur looks at the other boy like he must be kidding. "You still gotta pay the money?"

The other player nods and laughs. "That's way out!"

Coach Pingatore and his staff can see that Arthur is struggling in his new environment—on the court and off. "When Arthur first started at St. Joseph's," Pingatore remembers, "he was a good kid from what we saw, but he was very immature. He might have been a little more disruptive, speaking out, getting into childish things. He wasn't used to the discipline and control and the things we did here. He reverted back to, maybe, his environment, where he came from."

Arthur admits that he's having a tough time adjusting to the new school. "I just never been around a lot of white people. And it was different because at a black school, you know, I could associate with the people that . . . you know, they talk the way I talk. It's a little hard but I can adjust to it."

On the basketball court, Arthur does adjust. He wins the starting point guard position on the freshman team. The point guard is the player who brings the ball up the court, the player who controls the pace and strategy of the game. The coaches tell the rest of the team, "Get the ball to Arthur, because he's gonna do it for you." And sure enough, when the game is on the line, Arthur delivers.

Against Weber High School, Arthur gets the ball with less than twenty seconds left and the St. Joseph Chargers down by one point. He takes it upcourt quickly and makes a strong move to his left, dribbling through his legs. Then he cuts back to the right and drives into the heart of the key, dribbling with his left hand. For a split second he loses control, but he recovers and takes a soft, five-foot jump shot that bounces on the rim and falls through the hoop to give St. Joseph's the win. Arthur smiles proudly as his teammates surround him with high-fives and congratulations.

Arthur's freshman team finishes second in the conference. It's a good season, but not great. Still, Arthur looks forward to next year.

Back home in Garfield Park, Mrs. Agee notices some changes in her son. She feels like Arthur is growing up. Although she was originally concerned about him going to a strange school in the far-off suburbs, she now thinks it was a good idea. "I noticed the change immediately after he started going out there," Mrs. Agee explains. "To see your child mature, you think 'Oh! Maybe this is good for him.'"

Despite his new maturity and his successes on the basketball court, there's one area where Arthur doesn't make much progress during his freshman year—his schoolwork. By the end of the year, he's still working at a fourth or fifth grade level, and he's still in the lowest group of the general education program. Arthur is very honest about his attitude toward school. He doesn't like it.

"I don't think nobody in their right mind is crazy about school," he says. "If the President brought up a thing now to say, 'Close all schools,' do you think any kids would be trying to go out there, stand on a picket line and wave and get billboards saying, 'Reopen schools'?"

Arthur just shakes his head. No way.

• William's Freshman Year •

I think I may have seen the next Isiah Thomas. St. Joe's of Westchester has a kid named William Gates who is starting as a freshman.

—WILLIAM GLEASON, sportswriter

William Gates also feels out-of-place when he first attends St. Joseph's. "When I first came out here, it was like, boy, I wanna go home. Is this really the right school for me?

"Whatever little thing you do that goes against their rules, you have detention. And they'll suspend you quick at the school, too. They'll suspend you quick." William smiles as he thinks about just how quick they'll suspend a student at St. Joe's. Although the discipline is different from what he's used to, it's obvious that he respects it.

Like Arthur, William enters St. Joseph's working on a fourth or fifth grade level. And like Arthur, he never worried too much about school before. "Back in grammar school," he remembers, "academics didn't really matter too much to me at all. It was playing ball for the team . . . really, we were like the stand-outs in the school. If you showed up in class, that was good enough for them. I was just going to school for the girls, trip out with your friends, get out, go play some more basketball. That was basically it."

When William first showed his grammar school grades to his St. Joseph counselor, Sister Marilyn Hopewell, she was amazed by how bad they were. "You have to be one good ballplayer to get into school with these grades," she told him. A slight, soft-spoken black woman with a twinkle in her eyes, Sister Marilyn is unusual among the mostly white faculty of the school. She saw something special in William and developed a personal interest in his progress. "I could see that he had the potential," she explains, "but because he was shy, it seemed as though no one was trying to reach him."

With help from Sister Marilyn and with a new serious attitude toward school, William makes steady progress in his studies. "At the end of the year," she says with a smile, "he had gone four grades above where he started. Just in the way he listened and learned."

William's academic progress is only part of his successful freshman year. Coach Pingatore has made him a starting guard on the varsity basketball team, a team that's ranked #1 in the state of Illinois. Not even Isiah Thomas started as a freshman—although he was good enough. "I didn't do it," Pingatore explains, "because I was worried about bringing him along too rapidly. I think by not doing it cost us the state championship." Despite all his success, Gene Pingatore has never won the state championship, and he doesn't want to miss another opportunity. So he starts William as a freshman.

At practice Pingatore is tough and demanding with all his players, including William. During one scrimmage the coach screams at William to move faster. "Come to the ball! Come to the ball! Beat him, beat him, beat him . . . hold up. HOLD UP!"

Coach Pingatore stops the play and sticks his face about six inches away from William's. "You're killing us!" he shouts. "Why did he get to the ball before you?"

William doesn't answer. He just stares down at the wooden floor and listens. "He asks me do I want to be a great player," William explains later, "and I keep saying, 'Yeah.' He said, 'For four years I'm going to be on you every day, so you might as well get used to it now.'"

After the rest of the team has gone to the showers, Pingatore works with William individually. The coach has spotted a weakness in his young star's game—William is strong going to his right for a jump shot, but he's not as confident going to his left. So Pingatore has another player feed William the ball while William moves to his left and takes a quick jump shot. When William moves to his right by mistake, Pingatore shouts, "No! No! Hard left! Right—I know you can do it, left you can't. Hard. Go hard." This time William cuts to his left and takes the shot. It bounces off the rim, but Pingatore isn't worried about points right now; he's worried about the move. "Not bad," he says in a kinder voice. "Do it again."

Coach Pingatore's strategy with William seems to be paying off as the top-ranked Chargers dominate the regular season and power their way through the early stages of the play-offs. In Illinois, the play-offs are like a whole new season, with every team eligible to compete for a shot at the state championship. The losers are eliminated after each game, and the winners move on to face their next opponent.

In the sectional semifinals, William plays his best game of the season as St. Joseph's tough defense shuts down the team from Proviso East. Arthur is at the game as a spectator. His season is over now, but he gives William a big hug as the star player walks off the court. The next morning, William's picture is in the sports section of a Chicago newspaper.

In the sectional finals, Fenwick High School gives St. Joseph's their toughest test so far, taking a quick 10-2 lead in the first quarter. But in the second quarter, William takes charge. With his brother Curtis cheering him on from the stands, William scores sixteen points to lead the St. Joseph Chargers to the sectional title. From the smile on Curtis' face, it almost seems like it's Curtis himself who's out there starring on the court.

On a local television show called *Sportswriters on TV,* a well-known sportswriter named Bill Gleason makes a bold prediction: "I think I may have seen the next Isiah Thomas. St. Joe's of Westchester has a kid named William Gates who is starting as a freshman."

As the white-haired Gleason leans back in his chair and puffs on a big cigar, another cigar-smoking sportswriter chimes in: "Remember, you heard it first from Bill Gleason. . . . Put it in your memory banks . . . William Gates."

Now the winners of the sectional finals move on to another round of play called the supersectionals. The winners of the supersectionals will go to the state championship tournament at the University of Illinois in Champaign, located about 150 miles south of Chicago. People in the Chicago area call the Champaign area "downstate," and the dream of every Chicago area high school player is to go downstate for the tournament. William is caught up in the dream like anyone else would be. "Man, it'd be a big thing if I can go downstate as a freshman," he says.

In the supersectionals, St. Joseph's meets a tough

team from DeSales High School, led by Erik Anderson —a 6'9" senior who's been chosen a High-School All-American. For the first half, William plays more like an intimidated freshman than "the next Isiah Thomas." He's hesitant in his moves, and on one play, when he gets smashed across the nose by an elbow, he seems completely lost. In the meantime, Anderson dominates the Chargers on both ends of the court with blocked shots and thundering dunks.

Then, in the third quarter, William steps up and takes control. From deep in the left corner, he makes a beautiful arching jump shot over the outstretched arms of Anderson. Swish! Anderson fouls him on the shot, so William calmly steps to the line and sinks the free throw to turn it into a three-point play. Suddenly the Chargers are back on track.

Led by William's thirteen points in the second half, St. Joseph's pulls to within four points of DeSales with less than two minutes to play. It's a must-score situation, but the Chargers don't get the ball to William. The other St. Joseph's guard launches a long jump shot from the right corner, the ball bounces off the rim and DeSales grabs the rebound. They move the ball upcourt quickly for a lay-up that rolls off the front of the rim, and for a split second it looks like the Chargers still have a chance. But Erik Anderson comes flying downcourt to slam the missed lay-up through the hoop and put away the game.

As William walks off the court, Coach Pingatore pats the star freshman on the back before he slumps down onto the bench. It's a disappointing end to a great season. The Chargers won't be going downstate this year. But it's only the beginning for William Gates.

Paul Robert Walker

• Taking Care of Business •

I guess he thought I wasn't gonna be that big of a ball player. So why would he just waste some money on me staying there?

—ARTHUR AGEE

Before the next school year, St. Joseph's raises its tuition. William and Arthur both receive partial scholarships from the school, which cover some of their tuition. During his freshman year, the rest of William's tuition was paid by the C.Y.C.L.E. organization from Cabrini Green. But C.Y.C.L.E. can't pay for the increase in tuition, and William's mother can't pay for it either. Other students are faced with the same problem, so a fund-raiser named Brother Edwin Duprais tries to find additional sources of financial aid. Among the people he contacts is Patricia Wier, the president of Encyclopedia Britannica, one of the largest and most successful publishers of reference books in the world.

"I was called on by Brother Edwin Duprais," Mrs. Wier explains. "He was trying to raise money for kids who otherwise couldn't go to those kinds of schools. It really touched a soft spot in my heart, so I decided that my husband and I would participate on a personal basis. William was selected as the kid that was able to go to school based on our contribution."

Mrs. Wier takes a personal interest in William. She and her husband come to watch him play basketball, and they introduce him to their friends. William is very polite and grateful for their help. He knows that with support from Mrs. Wier, his entire education at St. Joseph's will be free.

Arthur Agee is a different story. During his freshman year, Arthur's family struggled to pay their portion of his tuition, and they still owed money by the end of the year. Now the tuition increase comes at a very bad time. Arthur's father has been laid off from a series of jobs, and he's out of work. "You look around your house," he says, "you see your food getting low, you know. You got the bills due here and your bills due there."

Brother Edwin Duprais and Coach Pingatore cannot find a generous person to help Arthur Agee. Instead, the school financial aid officer, Brother Leo, calls Arthur into his office and asks that his family pay a certain amount of what they owe or else Arthur can't come to school. When they can't pay the required amount, Arthur begins missing school for weeks at a time. Finally, when the Agee family owes $1,500 in back payments on tuition, Arthur is forced to leave St. Joseph's High School in the middle of the first semester of his sophomore year.

Mrs. Agee is disgusted with the coaches at St. Joseph's and the scouts like Earl Smith who come out to the inner city neighborhoods. She believes the scouts don't tell the whole truth when they recruit players like Arthur for their expensive suburban schools. "They offer them these scholarships," Mrs. Agee points out, "then once they get out there, the story is totally different. I was under the impression that Arthur would have help as far as getting to school. Arthur would have help as far as getting his books. Arthur would have help. . . . But see, none of that occurred."

Mrs. Agee's face draws tight with anger and frustration. "If I had known all of this was gonna lead to this, Arthur would have never gone to St. Joseph's."

Coach Pingatore believes it's just a question of money—pure economics. The school needs the tuition money to survive, and the Agee family can't pay. So Arthur has to leave. "By the end of the freshman year," he explains, leaning back in his chair, "whatever balance there was for tuition was never taken care of. Consequently, going into the sophomore year, we had the balance plus the new tuition, so it was going to continue to be a problem. You have to draw the line. Tuition is something that, as a school, we depend on for 90 percent of our revenue."

Arthur is devastated and depressed. His dream of following in the footsteps of Isiah Thomas seems to have vanished into the air. He believes it has nothing to do with tuition, and he doesn't really blame Earl Smith, either. He thinks it all comes down to basketball and physical size. Arthur is skinnier and shorter than William Gates, and he hasn't begun to develop the way William has.

"I thought Pingatore and the other coaches would help me out," Arthur says sadly, "but I guess he thought I wasn't gonna be that big of a ball player. So why would he just waste some money on me staying there, when you know, he thought I wasn't gonna grow. He kept on saying like, 'When you gonna grow?' or something like that. . . . Well, I don't know."

Arthur Agee never liked going to school, but now he

discovers that it isn't much fun being out of school. There isn't a lot to do around the Garfield Park neighborhood, and Mrs. Agee doesn't like her children spending time on the tough, dangerous streets. So Arthur hangs around the apartment, shooting baskets at the little hoop in his room with a nerf ball, or staring out the front window with his brother, Joe, watching the people and cars passing below. Sometimes he just closes his bedroom door and sits alone with his thoughts.

"He was so depressed and devastated," Mrs. Agee remembers, "he just closed himself off in the room, and I would go in there and I would tell him every day, 'Hey, things will look up.'"

Paul Robert Walker

• Marshall High •

In comparing Marshall High School to St. Joseph's, I don't think there is any comparison. . . . Our students, if they get out of high school, [for] a lot of them, it's an accomplishment.

—ARETHA MITCHELL, head counselor
at Marshall High School

After missing two months of classes, Arthur enrolls at the local public school, Marshall High. Right away, he realizes that Marshall is very different from St. Joseph's. The entrance to the suburban school was modern and open: a field of grass, clean light-colored bricks, and big glass windows that let the sun shine into the polished hallways. Like most Chicago schools, Marshall is a big, old, red-brick building set close to the city street, with dark, worn hallways that have seen thousands and thousands of students pass over the years.

Instead of the statue of St. Joseph that greets students at the suburban Catholic school, a beefy security guard checks the Marshall students for ID cards. One student shows up wearing a beeper, and the security guard demands that he surrender it. It's against the law for a student to take a beeper into school.

"Y'all can't take my beeper, man," the student protests.

The security guard calls over a second guard who also demands the beeper. "I'm gonna go, man," says the student.

"I know where you're gonna go," the guard tells him. "You're gonna go to jail. No beepers in here. Now don't make no scene." The security guard knows that a high school student who carries a beeper is probably a drug dealer. And there are plenty of drug dealers at Marshall High.

Arthur dresses differently at Marshall. He's back in his own world, with the black people that he knows, the people who "talk the way I talk." He wears flip-up sunglasses attached to his regular glasses, and keeps a quarter in his ear like a giant earring. Instead of the dress shirt and jeans he wore to St. Joseph's, he slips a loose-fitting, dark orange Atlanta Hawks jersey over a light orange T-shirt, and pulls on a pair of baggy sweatpants. On the outside, at least, he seems more relaxed. But there are problems and a deep hurt inside.

Arthur has lost a whole semester of credits while trying to clear up his financial problems at St. Joseph's. For a boy who struggles in his academic classes, that's an added burden. If he wants to graduate from high school after four years, he's going to have to make up those credits in summer school.

Marjorie Herd, a counselor at Marshall, understands Arthur's frustration. "Here you have a youngster caught in the middle of two separate school systems," she says. "Had he stayed at St. Joseph's, he would have been able to receive credit for the first semester. Doesn't seem fair, but then, that's the system."

Luther Bedford, the head basketball coach at Marshall, also understands the situation, but he thinks the real problem is not the two different school systems. Like Arthur, Coach Bedford believes it all comes down to basketball. "If he was going out there playing like they had predicted him to play, he wouldn't be at Marshall. Economics wouldn't have had anything to do with him not being at St. Joe's. Somebody would have made some kind of arrangement and the kid would have still been there."

A middle-aged black man with a deep, gravelly voice, Luther Bedford speaks with the same kind of confidence that Gene Pingatore has. He knows what he's talking about, and he's sure of what he's saying. But Coach Bedford doesn't have the same kind of financial support for his program that Coach Pingatore has at St. Joe's. He has to work with what he has, and he knows that sometimes the basketball team is the only thing that keeps a young man off the tough streets of Chicago.

"He's not making it like they thought he was gonna make it on the basketball court," Bedford continues, "so he's not there, simple as that. And it doesn't take no brilliant person to figure that out."

Arthur joins the sophomore team in mid-season. Coming off the bench as the sixth man, he makes an immediate impact with his ball-handling and hard-driving moves. At St. Joseph's, Arthur wore number ten. Now he wears number eleven—Isiah Thomas's number.

Arthur Agee is a strong young man. He's frustrated, and he's been hurt. But his hoop dreams are still alive.

School is a different matter. Arthur sits quietly at his desk and doesn't seem to pay much attention. In a history class, the teacher discusses the years after the American Civil War, when southern whites tried to take away the freedoms earned by the ex-slaves. She asks the class to name some of the techniques that whites used to keep blacks from voting.

A girl named Jeannetta raises her hand and suggests, "Poll tax."

The teacher nods and repeats the correct answer. The poll tax was a way of charging people money to vote. Today it's illegal, but after the Civil War the poll tax kept many poor black people from voting. Now the teacher turns to Arthur. "OK, Arthur, what other techniques were used to keep black Americans from voting?"

Arthur just smiles sheepishly and shakes his head. He has nothing to say, or perhaps he doesn't even hear the question.

"You could almost forget about his being there," the teacher says later, "that's how quiet he was initially. I think the transition had something to do with it."

Aretha Mitchell, the head counselor at Marshall, explains the difference between the two schools. "In comparing Marshall High School to St. Joseph's, I don't think there is any comparison. People can afford to send their children there [to St. Joseph's]. They can afford to put money into the school. Those students who go to St. Joseph's, once they walk in those doors, they walk in there to get that diploma and to go on to college. Whereas our students, if they get out of high school, [for] a lot of them, it's an accomplishment."

While Arthur struggles to adjust to the new school, the Agee family struggles at home. Mr. Agee is still out of work, and it hurts him that he wasn't able to help Arthur stay at St. Joseph's. "If he wants to go back next year, he's gonna go back if I have to beg," Mr. Agee says. "I wanna help him with his little dream."

Things turn even worse for the family when Mrs. Agee loses her job as a nurse's assistant because of chronic pain in her back. She has to rest her back as much as possible while also taking care of the children and the apartment. It's tough to live without money, very tough. And the strain takes a toll on Arthur's parents. After twenty years of marriage they begin to fight constantly, and Mr. Agee gradually turns to the drugs that are always waiting on the streets outside.

While her husband falls apart, Mrs. Agee struggles to protect her children from the dangerous life of the Chicago streets. "It's just a real hard area to live in," she says. "And as far as raising kids, kids don't even have a playground, a play area, or anything constructive to do in the neighborhood, so you see why half of them become gang-bangers. It's like you gotta keep your kids close to you and watch them at all times."

In the conflict between his parents, Arthur takes his mother's side. That spring, he writes her a beautiful letter for Mother's Day:

Dear Mother,
I hope when Mother's Day comes you will light up the sky with a big smile. You Mother are the only one in the world who can provide and take care of me. You are the one that makes our family work. You are the one that I will miss so much when I go away to college. No one can replace you ever.
Love, always,
Man

Man is a nickname that Arthur's father gave him when he was just a little boy. "That's Daddy's Man," Mr. Agee used to say, and the name stuck. But those days seem long ago now, and Arthur feels more and more distant from his father. So does the rest of the family. In June of 1989, just as Arthur finishes his sophomore year at Marshall High School, Mr. Agee walks out on his wife and three children.

• A Thoroughbred of a Player •

Seems like everybody I know is my coach.

—WILLIAM GATES

Like Arthur Agee, William Gates comes from a family with very little money. But William's brilliance on the basketball court has made it easier for him to go to an expensive private school like St. Joseph's. All of William's tuition, fees, books, and other educational needs are paid for, and he can concentrate on the two things that matter: his studies and his basketball.

William makes the most of his opportunity, working hard in his classes and on the court. The academic progress made during his freshman year continues into his sophomore year. In a math class, the teacher presents a difficult problem about writing an equation in scientific notation, a special form that scientists and mathematicians use to write very large or very small numbers. "Who wants this problem?" the teacher asks.

William's hand shoots up into the air. "Go ahead, William."

William carefully reads the answer he has written down. "Seven point three times ten to the third times ten to the negative second."

The math teacher nods and smiles enthusiastically. "Is that good?" he asks. "Very good."

Sitting at his desk, William beams with satisfaction. He knows he belongs in this class, belongs in this school. But it wasn't always that way. "When I went out there [to St. Joseph's]," he remembers, "I was very intimidated, 'cause I just knew that everybody out there was smarter than me. As the year went on, you know, I was making the A and B honor roll, and I felt like, hey, I was just as good as them."

On the basketball court, William is better than just as good. He is one of the best sophomore players in the state of Illinois—maybe in the nation. Coach Pingatore keeps working him hard in practice, and Curtis works him hard at home. Even watching TV becomes another form of basketball practice. One evening, Curtis and William are watching the Chicago Bulls play the Detroit Pistons on television. Curtis tells his younger brother to watch Bulls superstar Michael Jordan very carefully. It's not just the number of points he scores; it's how many shots he takes to score them.

"Make sure you look at how many shots [have] been taken," Curtis says. "Jordan might shoot fifteen out of forty."

"Fifteen out of forty!" William shakes his head as if Curtis is a little crazy. How could Michael Jordan take forty shots and only make fifteen of them?

"I'm just saying for instance," Curtis insists. "He's done it. But see, if you do that, you're gonna know about it." Curtis is trying to make William understand that he has to shoot more—even though Coach Pingatore's system limits his shots. Curtis wants William to use his own judgment about when to shoot and when not to shoot.

Mrs. Gates sits to the side of the living room, listening to her two sons discussing basketball. "Curtis said to William, 'The most important thing is getting the ball in the basket.' Curtis said the boy's good. He said he's real good, but he don't listen. He said if he listened to him he'd be better." She laughs out loud, thinking about how Curtis wasn't much for listening either.

Curtis Gates first went to Colby Junior College around the time that Michael Jordan arrived in the NBA. William remembers how Curtis and his friends would sit around and argue over who was best—Curtis or Michael Jordan. Maybe it was a silly argument, but Curtis Gates was definitely good—very good. He was named player of the decade at Colby College and received a scholarship to Central Florida. But Curtis didn't like being told what to do. He didn't get along with the coach and dropped out without getting his college diploma.

"Curtis's idea of being real good," Mrs. Gates explains, "is you don't follow the rules, you do what you want to do. Even if he didn't play ball, it was a nice university. He could have finished school. But he couldn't handle it." She shakes her head in sadness and frustration. Emma Gates values education, and she feels her older son lost a chance for a better life.

Curtis is frustrated, too. He's put on quite a bit of weight since his college days, though he still moves pretty well on the court. But without a degree, he can only get a low-paying job as a security officer at a local hospital, manning the security desk and issuing parking tickets to illegally parked cars.

"I'm used to everyone in the neighborhood loving me

and knowing how good I can play," he says. "It just seemed like people looked up to Curtis Gates when it came to basketball, but now I'm just a regular old guy on the street."

If Curtis's days of basketball greatness are over, William's are just beginning. Curtis knows that, and he wants to help William so much it almost makes him crazy. "All those basketball dreams I had, they're gone," Curtis admits. "All I see, all my dreams are in him now. I want him to make it so bad I don't know what to do."

William loves his older brother and respects his basketball knowledge. But he gets tired of being told what to do. "He's always telling me, 'You should do this and you should do that.' Seems like everybody I know is my coach."

For a fifteen-year-old boy, William Gates carries a lot of responsibility. He not only has his own hoop dreams, he carries the dreams of his brother Curtis and the dreams of Gene Pingatore. Coach Pingatore wants that state title, and he believes that William Gates is going to help get it for him.

Once again, the St. Joseph Chargers power their way through the early stages of the play-offs. In the sectional finals, featured as the Prep Game of the Week on local television, they face Gordon Tech—a suburban school with their own sophomore star, Tom Kleinschmidt. But in the first half it's all William Gates, as the young man from Cabrini Green pours in seventeen points to lead the Chargers.

"Gates . . . good!" shouts the television announcer, as William drives the baseline, fakes out a defender and puts the ball in the hoop. "Boy, Gates is on fire! William

Gates is one of the premier sophomores. . . . He is a thoroughbred of a player."

In the second half, however, Kleinschmidt steps up and sparks Gordon Tech to a slim lead. With twelve seconds left in the game and Gordon Tech up by three points, the St. Joseph Chargers have the ball. Coach Pingatore calls time-out to set up a play.

"Who do you go to?" asks the announcer. "If you got to have a three-pointer, my guy is William Gates. I'd like to see him get it, just get to go one-on-one, pull up and ice it. Oh boy, let's see what they do in these last twelve seconds. This is it! The sectional championship!"

Sure enough, just as the announcer predicted, the Chargers get the ball to William Gates. He dribbles quickly up the left side of the court and pulls up for a long jump shot from five feet beyond the three-point line. But the shot is too quick and too long. The ball bounces off the front of the rim, and the players in the middle bat it around. Another Charger finally grabs control, dribbles out to the three-point line, and rushes a desperation shot with three seconds left. It's no good, either.

"Gordon Tech wins!" the announcer shouts. "Congratulations to the Gordon Tech Rams. They're on a joyride—one game now from Champaign."

William Gates shuffles off the court with his eyes to the floor. He played a brilliant game, but he missed the one shot they needed to keep the dream alive. His dream. Curtis's dream. Coach Pingatore's dream. Once again, the hoop dreams will have to wait until next year.

• Sophomore Summer •

You got old legs, Dad, old legs.

—ARTHUR AGEE, summer of 1989

William Gates walks through the crowded streets of downtown Chicago. He looks clean and neat, wearing a dress shirt and tie, a good pair of slacks, a baseball jacket, and a baseball cap. It's June, and the early morning sun filters down through the tall buildings while a cool breeze blows off Lake Michigan. William enters a large building, rides the elevator upward, and shows his ID card outside an automatic glass door. Then he steps inside and goes to work.

During the summer following his sophomore year, William works for Encyclopedia Britannica, filing big spools of computer tape that contain millions of bits of information. It's an excellent job for a sixteen-year-old boy with no experience, but William was offered the job by Mrs. Wier, the president of the company who is also helping to pay for his school expenses.

"I said to him, what are you going to do this summer?" Mrs. Wier explains. "And he said, well, he didn't know. So I said, if you need a job let me know and I'll see if I can help you. We had a job that didn't require a lot of previous training, so we hired him."

William appreciates the opportunity, just as he appreciates Mrs. Wier's help with his education. He takes the job seriously and does his best to do it right. But at first he finds the work difficult and confusing.

"I messed up so bad on my first day," he admits. "Just messed up everything. Putting tapes in the wrong numbers and all sorts of stuff."

But William doesn't get discouraged. He keeps coming to work every day, listening and learning the same way he listened and learned when he first came to St. Joseph's. And as the summer progresses, he becomes more confident. He's proud that he can handle a job in the real business world, and he's especially proud that he can help his mother.

"I just push myself to come out here," he says, "because I know in the long run it's going to be good for myself and for my family. I give my mother fifty dollars out of my checks. All she's done for me, I don't think there will ever be enough that I can get to pay her back . . ." William pauses for a moment and flashes a small smile, as if he's almost embarrassed to admit his dream out loud, "unless I make pro—then I'm pretty sure I can pay her back."

No one offers Arthur Agee a summer job. He spends his mornings in summer school trying to make up the credits he missed because of his problems at St. Joseph's. And he spends his afternoons playing basketball on the inner city playgrounds.

Arthur has grown during his sophomore year— inside and outside. Inside, he has a new confidence. He made it through the difficult change from St. Joseph's to Marshall, and he proved himself on the sophomore team. Now he has high hopes of starting on the varsity team during his junior year.

Arthur has grown outside as well. He's still skinny, but his shoulders are broader and he's much taller—about six feet. Not exactly a giant, but big enough for a high school point guard. And almost as big as Isiah Thomas.

One afternoon Arthur and a group of young men from the neighborhood play a fast-paced, full-court game at a school playground. Arthur wears a red and white basketball uniform that he got from a special tournament. On the front of the uniform the white letters say: "Push Excel Pro Basketball Classic." On the back of the uniform it says, "Thomas 11." For Arthur Agee, the dream of following Isiah Thomas is still alive.

Arthur pushes the ball downcourt, dribbles behind his back, and nails a long jump shot. Later, the players take a break from their game and Arthur shows off a new skill he has developed. Dribbling toward the basket, he takes off from his left foot, flies through the air as if gravity doesn't matter, and slams the ball through the basket. In a real game, a point guard like Arthur doesn't need to slam-dunk, but it makes him feel good to do it, and it's fun to show off for this friends.

Suddenly, Mr. Agee shows up on the playground. His chest is bare above his sweatpants, and he looks thinner, like he hasn't been eating regularly. Arthur doesn't see his father much these days, and there is an uncomfortable feeling in the air as they give each other a quick hug. Arthur is almost as tall as Mr. Agee now, and he wants to show him what he can do.

"Watch this," he says. "Watch this dunk." Arthur dribbles the ball—once, twice, three times—then he takes off from his left foot and slams it through the hoop.

Paul Robert Walker

Mr. Agee smiles as he watches his oldest son, but the smile is tired and distant. "Joe, I'm going after you, okay?" He's talking to Arthur but he calls him by the wrong name, confusing him with his youngest son, Joseph.

Now Mr. Agee tries to dunk. He takes a quick, awkward left-handed dribble, switches the ball to his right hand and takes off weakly toward the basket. But he can barely bring the ball up to the bottom of the rim. It's not even close.

"You got old legs, Dad," says Arthur with a laugh, pulling up his baggy uniform shorts. "Old legs."

Mr. Agee laughs, too, and begins to walk away. "Hey, Man, I'll see you later on, okay?"

Arthur nods and finishes tightening his shorts. But he can't help noticing his father, standing on the far side of the playground and waving money in his hand. A few other men are hanging out near a small, broken-down wooden building that stands in the shadow of the big brick school. When they see the money, one of the men disappears behind the building while Mr. Agee waits and the other men stand guard. Then the first man returns, takes the money from Mr. Agee, and hands him a small package.

From the other side of the playground, Arthur sees everything. He doesn't say a word, and his face shows no emotion. But his eyes flash with anger and frustration. He knows his father is buying drugs.

At home, Mrs. Agee struggles to keep her family fed and clothed. Arthur is old enough to understand his mother's problems, and he appreciates everything she does for him. He knows that it's his mother who keeps the family going. But something else keeps Arthur going, too—his hoop dreams.

He covers his bedroom walls with photos of Isiah Thomas, and when he is not wearing the red and white "Thomas" uniform, he hangs it on the wall along with the photos. He puts up a homemade Detroit Pistons banner, and he cuts out an article about a new sixteen million-dollar contract that Thomas has recently signed. When he finds out that Isiah Thomas was once nicknamed "Tuss," he starts calling himself Tuss. He even writes the name on his basketball shoes, and proudly shows them to a visitor. "I drew on these," he says, "Look at my name: Tuss. Say Tuss."

Arthur laughs and does a series of muscle-man poses in a gray Georgetown basketball jersey. What's the number on the jersey? Number eleven, of course. He knows it's all a little silly, but he can't help himself. All he thinks about is following in Isiah's footsteps and making it from the streets of west Chicago to the NBA.

Mrs. Agee wants Arthur to be more realistic. "Man, you may not make it to the NBA," she cautions him.

But Arthur doesn't want to hear about it. "Don't keep on telling me things like that. That's just like showing me that you don't have any trust in what I do."

"I do," Mrs. Agee explains, "but don't keep putting everything into this."

Arthur just shakes his head. "Ain't nobody gonna take my dream away from me. That's what I want to be and that's what I'm gonna do."

Mrs. Agee shrugs her shoulders and smiles. "Hey, it's your dream. What can we do?"

Later, Arthur plays nerf basketball in his bedroom

with his brother, Joe. He fakes the younger boy out and flies across the room for a thundering dunk through the tiny hoop. For a moment—in the world of his imagination and dreams—Arthur Agee is playing in the NBA.

• The Next William Gates •

You want to go downstate? You got to do something about it.

—COACH PINGATORE, to William Gates

William Gates wants to play in the NBA just as much as Arthur Agee does. But William doesn't wear Isiah Thomas's uniform or write Isiah's nickname on his basketball shoes. In fact, as he begins his third season on the varsity team, William admits that he's tired of hearing about Isiah Thomas. Even Coach Pingatore's mother, who works in the school lunchroom, keeps talking about the former St. Joseph's star.

"Did you see Isiah play last night?" she asks William. "How'd you like it?"

William smiles politely. "Yeah, I caught that. He played pretty good." Later, William expresses his frustration. "The whole school sees me as being an Isiah Thomas. I'm trying to build my own identity. When I leave they can say, 'You're gonna be the next William Gates.'"

No one knows who "the next William Gates" might be, but the original William Gates is attracting plenty of attention from top colleges around the country. Some college coaches actually began writing to William during his freshman year, but now, as he moves into the second half of his high school career, he's flooded with hundreds of recruitment letters.

"Any school you name!" William exclaims, flipping through stacks of letters and brochures in his family's Cabrini Green apartment. Picking up one letter, he reads, "Dear William: Georgetown University basketball staff is very interested in you." Another letter begins, "We're going to kick off the season with a midnight madness celebration." William smiles and arches his eyebrows—he likes the sound of that midnight madness.

"Bobby Knight called," he says, referring to the legendary coach of Indiana University. "Michigan State called, too—boy did they ever call!" A letter from the University of Iowa advises him, "Catch the Hawkeyes on TV; we'll be on national television." Another letter promises more than television: "Dear William," he reads, "There's gold at the end of the rainbow. Five hundred dollars in there for you, too." William pretends to look in the envelope for the money, and laughs when he doesn't find it. The letter doesn't really promise five hundred dollars; that's just William's joke. But the gold at the end of the rainbow is real—for the handful of players who make it to the NBA.

Although the major colleges are already beating on his door, William still has plenty of work left in high school. Coach Gene Pingatore knows that better than anyone. Coach Pingatore has always given William special attention, but now there's a subtle change in the way he treats his star. William Gates is no longer the freshman sensation or the super sophomore, no longer the young player whom Pingatore has to whip into shape. Now William is a mature young man, a team leader. In his first two seasons, William played the off-guard position—the "shooting" guard. But this year, Coach Pingatore is moving him to point guard. It's William's team now.

One afternoon Pingatore and William sit together, watching a videotape of Isiah Thomas from back when the Detroit superstar played for St. Joseph's. Although the coach uses this time as a teaching session, he talks to William with a new respect—almost as though they are equals, two grown men sitting together and planning their strategy for the coming season.

"Watch Isiah," Pingatore says, puffing on his pipe. "Watch him come. What'd he do?"

"Took a charge," William answers with a small smile.

"He took the charge." Coach Pingatore punches his player affectionately on the shoulder. "Something we have to get you to do, right?"

William smiles again. "Yeah."

On video, the announcer praises Isiah to the sky. "Everything he does is what a coach is looking for. . . ."

Pingatore glances at William. "You listening?"

William nods, never taking his eyes off the screen. As the two watch more of Isiah, Coach Pingatore pays William a surprising compliment. "You're actually a better shooter than Isiah from the outside." William looks at the coach as if he must be kidding. But Pingatore nods his head seriously. "True," he says. For a moment, the teacher and student continue to watch the game in silence. Then Coach Pingatore hits William with the real point of the session. "That means you have a lot of responsibility, William. Can you handle it?"

"I hope so," William replies. "I'm ready to go downstate."

"You want to go downstate?" Pingatore asks, not waiting for an answer. "You got to do something about it. You've got two years to get us down there, and it's going to be all on your head."

In practice, Coach Pingatore still drives William hard, but there's a new respect there as well. He's no longer screaming at William for not hustling; now he just wants his star to step up and take control.

One day William brings the ball upcourt on a fast break. When the defense leaves the middle wide open, he passes to another player who misses a twelve-foot jump shot from the right side.

"Hold up!" Pingatore shouts. As the players stop in their tracks, the coach approaches his star. He doesn't scream in the young man's face like he did when William was a freshman. Now he gives William a little space, and his voice is calmer, almost pleading with him to do it right. "William, the man playing defense dropped way off here. Now who would you rather have shoot the ball?" Pingatore points to the other player who missed the shot. "Stras shoot the ball there, or you stop in here and shoot the ball?"

William mutters that he should shoot it himself.

"Well, shoot it!" Pingatore exclaims.

As the practice continues, Coach Pingatore notices that William is playing cautiously. It's his first day back after recovering from a slight knee injury, and he seems to be afraid to go hard on the knee. "Come on, let's go!" Pingatore shouts. "William, you're playing soft. Does it bother you? Don't be afraid though, don't favor it."

At the end of practice, Pingatore makes the team run wind sprints, a standard training exercise that builds endurance. As the players run at full speed from one end of the court to the other and back, the coach times them on the wire-caged gym clock, determined to make them run until they go up and back in ten seconds. William is normally one of the fastest players on the team, but now he lags behind the others, and Pingatore doesn't include him in the ten-second requirement.

As the players cross the baseline and grab their knees to catch their breath, Pingatore looks up at the clock and shakes his head in disgust. "Nope. We'll stay here all day until you get a ten second one. William, you got to take it easy." The coach blows the whistle to start another sprint. "Go!" Another sprint. "Go!" Another. "Go!" Again and again the team fails to make it in ten seconds. "Now we start all over," Pingatore informs them. "You people just refuse to work."

After practice, the players sit in the grandstands as Coach Pingatore bellows out his disgust. "You don't know what it is to be intense!" he shouts. "And if you don't have it, you're going to be crap for this team!"

The players are obviously exhausted from the wind sprints—red faced, sweaty, and out of breath. But Pingatore isn't through with them. He picks out individual players for special criticism. "Give me a good reason why I should keep you on this team, Corey. How about you, Reed? Give me a good reason."

Now he turns to William, but his voice is different, gentler, more reasonable. It's almost as if Pingatore and William are on one side and the rest of the players are on the other side. "What do you think, William?" the coach asks. "I mean how many of these people work hard?"

William shifts uncomfortably in his seat. He doesn't like being put in the position of criticizing his teammates. Finally he whispers, "Not too many."

"Not too many," Pingatore repeats, loudly so everyone can hear it. "You want to stay home when the state tournament comes?" he asks the team. No one answers. Pingatore turns away in disgust. "All right, go on in."

The next day, William reinjures his knee during practice. He goes to an orthopedic specialist named Dr. Wolin who examines the knee and has it X-rayed and tested for strength and motion. When the results are in, Dr. Wolin explains the situation. The doctor is a slightly-built man with a trim beard and kind, caring eyes. He speaks calmly and soothingly, but he doesn't pull any punches.

"You most likely have at least torn this cartilage," Dr. Wolin begins, showing William a plastic model of the knee joint. "The inside cartilage of your knee. And you may have a ligament tear in your knee, okay? If the ligament is torn, William, you would miss this year entirely. This is a lot to happen to you at an early age, but I think if all goes well you'll be able to come back."

William listens to the news somberly, struggling to keep his emotions under control. When the doctor is gone, he sits on the edge of the examining table, playing with the plastic knee model. He doesn't cry, but the tears are there, waiting inside. "Everything was just going great," he says quietly. "Now this."

• Something to Keep His Spirit Up •

Our lights were cut off, our gas was cut off, and we were sitting in the dark.

—Mrs. Sheila Agee

During his junior year, Arthur makes the varsity team for the Marshall Commandos. On picture day, the players swarm into Coach Bedford's cramped office to pick up their uniforms. Everyone wants a large uniform so they can sport the baggy look made famous by NBA players like Michael Jordan. But there aren't enough large uniforms to go around.

Luther Bedford is a weary veteran coach of the Chicago Public School system. For over twenty years he has had to patch together a basketball squad on Marshall's meager athletic budget. With no real assistant coach or team manager to help, the task of distributing Marshall's preciously few uniforms falls to him.

"All you guys can't get large!" Coach Bedford exclaims in frustration. "Somebody got to wear a medium. You little skinny guys want to get the large. What are the other guys going to put on?"

Arthur doesn't worry so much about the size of the uniform. What really matters to him is the number. He smiles proudly when he grabs number eleven—Isiah's number. In fact he's so happy, he has to shout it out loud so everyone can hear, "Number eleven!"

Out on the court, the players pose for the school's photography teacher, Ada Kolmodin. She uses a regular camera and flash unit, unlike the professional equipment used for St. Joseph's team pictures. When they line up for the team photo, Ms. Kolmodin asks them, "Is this the year?" They each hold up a finger to show that Marshall is number one.

After the team photo, she sets up the individual photos, with each player standing on the top of a desk, so she can shoot him holding a ball high above the basket. Arthur flashes a big grin for the camera. He is obviously enjoying himself, and he looks good in his gold and burgundy uniform. He's proud that he made the varsity, proud to be wearing number eleven. After Ms. Kolmodin snaps his photo, he leaps from the desk and slams the ball through the hoop.

At home, things aren't going so well for Arthur and his family. Still unable to work because of her back pain, and without any support from her husband, Mrs. Agee has been forced to go on welfare. Some people believe welfare is a free ride—that it's easier to live on welfare than work. But Mrs. Agee knows better.

"Trying to live month to month on something like that is very hard," she explains, her arms crossed tightly. "And you have three growing kids that need this and you have bills to pay. It's just not enough to make ends meet."

Mrs. Agee pauses for a moment and struggles to control her emotions. It's not only hard for her to live on welfare, it's embarrassing and frustrating. "I was never raised on welfare," she points out. "My mother and father both worked."

Mrs. Agee always worked, too, until she lost her job

because of her back. And Mr. Agee worked until he got laid off from a series of jobs and couldn't find a new one. Maybe it was the frustration of being unemployed that drove him out into the streets. It's hard to say. But the truth is that the Agee family used to be better off than many people in the inner city. They're not anymore. When a family has to depend on welfare, it's like being a fly in a spider's web. They become caught up in a big government system that treats people like numbers instead of human beings. It's a system without a heart.

"We were cut off for three months," Mrs. Agee explains. "We were cut off Aid completely with no income. So therefore, do you know what happened? Our lights were cut off, our gas was cut off, and we were sitting in the dark." During this period the only light in the apartment came from a single lamp that was connected to a long extension cord the Agees had hooked up to the downstairs apartment.

For a mother of three children, Mrs. Agee still looks pretty and young, wearing gold hoop earrings and a blue and red Detroit Pistons sweatshirt. But her voice is weary. "They cut me off because I failed to meet an appointment. It hurt everybody in here. It changed everybody's attitude that you can have something today, and it's gone tomorrow.

"So you know what the system is saying to me?" she asks, her deep brown eyes flashing with anger. "Do you know what it's saying to a lot of women in my predicament? They don't care."

As the year goes on, Mrs. Agee has two more children to look after. Arthur's sister, Tomika, gives birth to a baby girl named Jazz. The father is away in a Navy training program, so Jazz and her mother join the Agee household.

Around the same time, Arthur's friend Shannon moves in with the Agees to escape the problems in his own family. Shannon is a handsome, bright young man with an athletic build similar to Arthur's, and the two share a deep, caring friendship. They do everything together—go to school together, play basketball together, and hang out together afterward.

"Shannon is like me," Arthur says. "He understood me and I understood him."

Shannon feels the same way about Arthur. "He could sit back and talk to me because I was his best friend. He trusted me and I trusted him."

One evening, Shannon and the Agees sit around the kitchen table for dinner. All they've got to eat are hot dogs split open on white bread and smeared with mustard, and instant noodles on the side. The three older children talk about how things will be different when they go to college.

"Y'all get your own place," says Mrs. Agee.

Shannon's eyes light up. "Yeah! We can all go to Arby's, baby!"

"And get fresh Matt's cookies!" says Arthur, reaching across the table to grab Shannon's hand in a finger-snapping handshake.

"And go into Jewel's for our meat!" Shannon adds, thinking about all the delicious meat waiting at the big grocery store.

Tomika stands behind the table, making more hot dog sandwiches on the kitchen counter. "That take a lot of food stamps," she points out. Food stamps are special stamps that people on welfare use to buy food, and at the moment that's the only way Tomika can imagine shopping at the grocery store. But Shannon doesn't want to hear about it.

"We ain't gonna need no food stamps," he says.

After dinner, the young people eat popsicles while Mrs. Agee looks at Arthur's homework paper and holds it up proudly for everyone to see. "That is so neat. That is what you call a neat paper."

"No it's not," Shannon teases her. "He copied it!"

Arthur laughs. "Why you lie?" he asks good-naturedly. He knows he didn't copy the paper and Shannon knows it, too.

"Now don't you say that about my son," Mrs. Agee demands. "My son got a brain."

"But he don't use it!" Shannon exclaims.

Although Shannon pokes fun at Arthur, it's obvious that he really cares about his friend. He understands what Arthur is going through during the break-up of his parents' marriage, because Shannon went through the same painful experience himself. It was bad enough when Mr. Agee walked out on the family, but he doesn't leave them alone.

"It's been crazy as far as his father and his mother's break-up," Shannon explains. "He'll come home, you know, and Bo's stealing, buying drugs, and beating on his mother and stuff."

Mrs. Agee finally has to call the police and get a legal order to protect herself from Mr. Agee. He's convicted of battery, which is a legal term for assaulting someone physically. Later, he's convicted of burglary and sentenced to the county jail.

"My father was the same way," Shannon says. "I think about it all the time. When you come home and they're fighting, you know that gets to a child's head. Especially when you're living with your mother and you're young, and that's all you see, all the time."

Shannon knows that it's getting to Arthur's head, too. And he understands that Arthur needs something good in his life, something to help him make it through this painful time. "He had to do something to keep his spirit up."

Fortunately, Arthur Agee does have something to keep his spirit up. It's called basketball.

• Under the Knife •

When basketball is over, William may not have a friend in the world.

—CURTIS GATES

William Gates lays flat on a moving table and lifts his head slightly to see where he's going. Like a conveyer belt, the table carries his body slowly into a plastic tunnel—part of a million-dollar medical machine that can make images of the soft tissues of the body. A regular X-ray machine clearly shows problems in the hard structures, like broken bones. But it only hints at problems in soft structures like cartilage and ligaments. This machine, called a Magnetic Resonance Imaging machine—or MRI for short—can show Dr. Wolin exactly what's wrong with William's knee.

Once inside the tunnel, William lays back and closes his eyes. He tries to fight claustrophobia, the panicky feeling some people get when they're stuck in a very small space. Then the clicking starts—a series of loud, rapid clicks that seem to go on forever. These clicks are radio pulses that work with the magnetic field to make the images. While William lies inside the plastic tunnel, a medical technician and a doctor called a radiologist sit at a computerized control board, watching the images and making adjustments.

Later, Dr. Wolin explains the results of the test as William sits nervously in a straight-backed chair. "The good news is that your ligament looks fine," he begins.

William breaks into a big smile. He's so excited that he bends over from his waist and practically touches his knees with his forehead. But the doctor continues speaking in a calm, steady voice.

"Okay. Your ligament looks fine," he repeats. "I think that we can actually sew the cartilage back. So you're looking at a minimum of twelve weeks, maybe sixteen weeks, before I let you play ball again."

Suddenly William's smile disappears and he nervously fingers his lower lip. Twelve to sixteen weeks is a long time to be out of the line-up, a long time to go without basketball.

"Possibly being able to play by tournament time," Dr. Wolin continues. "Okay?"

William doesn't say anything. The regular season hasn't even started yet, and tournament time seems a long way off. It's not okay. But at least he has a chance to play again this year.

A few days later, William is wheeled into the operating room on a rolling cart. He wears a white hospital gown and a blue paper hat to cover his hair. A plastic bag full of fluid hangs on a metal pole attached to the cart. A plastic tube leads down from the bag into a needle, which is inserted into a vein on top of William's hand. This system is called an IV, short for intravenous, because it delivers substances directly into the vein.

As he enters the operating room, William is nervous—very nervous. A doctor called an anesthesiologist leans over him and says in a very calming voice, "I'm going to slip you a little something into the IV to kind of take the edge off of things. OK? All right?"

William just nods. The "little something" is medicine to make him more relaxed. A short while later, William can feel the medicine working. "I can tell," he says with a sleepy smile. "I can tell."

Next the anesthesiologist puts a mask over William's face and asks him to breathe deeply. The mask delivers a gas that will put William to sleep for the surgery. A few minutes later, William is completely unconscious, with plastic tubes sticking out of his mouth to maintain a flow of oxygen and drain extra saliva.

Now Dr. Wolin begins the surgery. First he makes a small cut in William's right knee. It's only an inch or so long, but it's big enough for the blood to flow freely down William's leg. Next, the doctor inserts a thin metal tube called an arthroscope through the cut. The arthroscope is an amazing medical instrument that allows Dr. Wolin to see and work inside William's knee. The images from within the knee appear magnified on a video screen in the operating room, and the doctor actually watches what he's doing on the screen rather than looking at it directly in the knee. An arthroscope usually allows the doctor to perform surgery with only one or two small cuts in the knee, but in William's case, Dr. Wolin also makes a longer four-inch cut below the knee in order to sew the damaged cartilage back together.

While Dr. Wolin cuts and probes within William's knee, Mrs. Gates sits in the waiting room. An old song by the Carpenters plays quietly over the speakers. Her eyes are tired and her face is drawn tight with nervousness. She knows that William is receiving the best medical care available and the entire cost of his surgery is being paid by the school's insurance. But Dr. Wolin

Paul Robert Walker

has given her a more cautious timetable for William's recovery, and she's concerned about how this surgery will affect her son's chances to make his hoop dreams come true.

"The doctor told me he wouldn't even try to get him ready to play this year," she says. "What do you think that will do to his career?"

Mrs. Gates doesn't wait for an answer to her question. She thinks about her older son and the disappointments in his basketball career. "I really thought Curtis was gonna make it. But he didn't make it. So I . . ." She manages a weak smile before finishing her sentence. "I just wanted this one to make it."

After the surgery, William lays in the recovery room until the effects of the anesthesia begin to wear off. When he regains consciousness, Dr. Wolin leans over him to report on the results of the surgery. "We were able to repair the cartilage," the doctor says confidently. "We're right on the schedule we talked about."

William can barely open his eyes, and he doesn't feel awake enough yet to speak. He just nods slightly to show the doctor that he understands.

Mrs. Gates isn't the only one worried about William. His brother Curtis is worried, too. He knows from personal experience how quickly life can change once you're no longer a basketball star. "When basketball is over," he says, "William may not have a friend in the world."

Curtis has lost his job as a security officer, and he's been out of work for over four months. Without a college degree or special training, he knows he's going to have a hard time finding a good job. One afternoon, a few weeks after William's surgery, Curtis works on his car on the street outside Cabrini Green. He's bundled up against the cold Chicago winter, wearing a T-shirt, a work shirt, a hooded sweatshirt, and a black jacket. The layers of clothing make Curtis look even heavier than usual, and his days of basketball stardom seem lost in the past. All he has to remind him of those days on the court is the license plate on his car: C GATES 1. He got the plate when he felt like someone special. But he doesn't feel very special anymore.

"My life ain't got no better since I stopped playing ball," Curtis admits sadly. "I just went down, down. Sometimes I sit around and my eyes kind of get watery—like I ain't amounting to nothing. I ain't got nothing. I can't even go out there and get a job making seven dollars an hour, you know."

Later, Curtis sits on the low brick wall of a local shopping center, watching the people pass by. He is still bundled against the cold, still feeling discouraged about his life. "I'll be sitting there telling myself, you ain't gonna get no better."

Curtis is only in his early twenties, but he feels like he missed his chance to be somebody. Curtis doesn't want William to miss his.

• He Earned His Title •

I look up on the scoreboard, my name is not even on there anymore. Where do I fit in with this team?

—WILLIAM GATES

After he is released from the hospital, William works out every day at the YMCA near his home. It takes hours and hours of hard, painful work to come back from knee surgery and play basketball. Under the watchful eye of a physical therapist, he rides a stationary bicycle, trying to pedal faster and harder each day. He works on a special weight machine, grunting in pain as he strengthens the muscles around his knee. And when the riding and weightlifting are over, he swims lap after lap alone in the blue-green water of the indoor pool.

The hard training is only one of the changes in William's life. The previous spring, his girlfriend, Catherine, gave birth to a baby girl named Alicia. At the age of sixteen, William Gates is a father.

Alicia was born the day after St. Joseph's lost to Gordon Tech in the state tournament, and at first William tried to keep the baby a secret from Coach Pingatore and the rest of the staff at St. Joe's. "I was just basically scared to tell people," he admits. "I was feeling sick holding all this stuff inside of me and I couldn't let it out. When I finally did tell coach, he was like, 'When did this come about?' And I said, 'You know, three or four months ago!'" William laughs when he thinks about Coach Pingatore's surprise. But he laughs even more when he plays with Alicia. She's no longer a newborn; now she's a cute, cuddly baby, sitting comfortably in Catherine's arms and giggling when William offers her a pacifier.

William was in the delivery room when Alicia was born. "The nurses gave her to Catherine," he remembers, "and she handed the baby to me. I know one thing —I'll never forget how hard she was squeezing my hand." William breaks into a warm, happy smile at the memory. It's different than his smiles on the basketball court. Alicia is something more than basketball. She's a tiny person who is part of him. Many teenage fathers run away from their responsibilities, but William takes his responsibility to Alicia seriously. Before he could act like Alicia's father, though, he had to prove himself to Catherine.

"Once we got her home," Catherine explains, "William offered his help and stuff, but it was almost like I didn't want it because she was mine, you know, instead of the two of us. So then, after a while, I finally let him keep her." Catherine smiles warmly, too. "He earned his title."

"Felt good," says William proudly. He holds a small teddy bear in his hand and shakes it gently in front of Alicia's face, drawing a high-pitched baby giggle. Then he does it again for more giggles. And again. And again. Finally, Alicia takes the teddy bear in her tiny hands and gives it a kiss.

After weeks of hard work at the YMCA, William returns to Dr. Wolin's office for an examination. Just as he did when William first came to see him after the injury, the doctor has the knee tested for strength and movement with special equipment. Afterwards, William lays back on the examining table, nervously fingering the scar on his knee as he waits for the doctor to discuss the results.

"Your numbers look good," Dr. Wolin reports, eliciting a smile from William that's almost as big as the smile he gives Alicia. "I think you're two or three weeks away from being able to practice full. You know what I mean?"

William's smile drops away and he sits up halfway on the table, leaning on his elbow. He is obviously disappointed. "Two or three weeks," he says. But he makes it sound like two or three years.

Dr. Wolin understands William's frustration. "I know you wanted to waltz in here today, and I'd tell you to go back to practice right now. I don't want it to have to tear again."

Even with William out of the line-up, St. Joseph rolls through the regular season. Another guard has taken William's place, and he's doing an excellent job—not quite as good as William perhaps, but good enough to produce a winning season. As his teammates run up and down the floor, William watches from the stands, wearing his red letterman's sweater with a big "J" for St. Joseph's. When the team scores, he applauds politely, but his handsome face shows the strain and the hurt he feels inside. He doesn't want to watch; he wants to play.

"I felt that this was the year for me," he says quietly. "I know we can make it downstate. That's just a big dream I had." William gazes up at the scoreboard. He recognizes every name, every number. But there's one name and number that isn't there: 22 Gates. "I look up on the scoreboard, my name is not even on there anymore. Where do I fit in with this team?"

William's frustration over basketball begins to affect his schoolwork. "When I stopped playing basketball," he admits, "all my grades just sunk."

On the day of the semester final exam in Algebra II, William doesn't show up. Later, his teacher allows him to take a makeup exam. During the fall, William was doing extremely well in the challenging math class. But now, as he takes the exam, he finds it difficult to concentrate. He hasn't really been studying the way he should, and the old confidence is gone.

After the teacher has graded the exam, he explains the results to William. "Here's the cut-off point for passing," he says, pointing to a list of grades, "and you ended up right there. So you passed the final, barely. . . ." The teacher smiles at William, but it's a sad sort of smile. Everyone likes William Gates. He's not only the school's star basketball player, he's the kind of person who other students want to be friends with, the kind of person who teachers enjoy having in class. But the math teacher knows that William is not working up to his ability anymore. He's struggling and barely getting by.

The math test is important, but there's another test that's more important to William's future. It's called the ACT, which stands for American College Testing program. The ACT is one of two tests that colleges use in selecting students for admission. (The other test is called the SAT, which stands for Scholastic Aptitude Test.) The ACT tests a student's ability in various subject areas, including vocabulary, reading comprehension, and mathematics. The scores in these areas are combined into a single score called a composite. In order for William to accept an athletic scholarship at a four-year university, he has to have a composite score of eighteen. But when he first takes the test in his junior year, he only scores a fifteen.

After receiving his test results, William meets with Coach Pingatore to discuss the situation. He hands the coach the paper detailing his scores and sits uncomfortably in front of Pingatore's big desk while the coach scans the numbers. Pingatore has seen plenty of low scores before, so he's not exactly shocked. But he can't hide the disappointment in his voice. Just a few months earlier, William had been getting As and Bs in his schoolwork.

"Not as good as we wanted, huh?" Pingatore says finally.

William just nods. He isn't too happy about the situation, either.

"I think what we have to do is get you set up with the Britannica course," Coach Pingatore continues, a little more enthusiasm in his voice. "We'll have to talk to Mrs. Wier."

The Britannica course is a special six-week class that teaches students how to improve their test scores. It doesn't try to teach all the information that might appear on the test; that would be impossible, because the information takes years to learn. Instead, the course makes students more comfortable with the whole idea of taking tests, and it teaches various test-taking techniques that usually produce higher scores.

The Britannica course is taught at a special learning center run by the Encyclopedia Britannica. The course is expensive, but William's sponsor, Mrs. Wier, allows William to take the course for free. Every day after school, he sits at a long table with another student, taking practice tests and listening to the teacher explain some of the ways to improve his scores.

The teacher shows William that his first instinct is usually better than trying to second-guess himself. "Sometimes you had the right answer," she points out, "and you changed it to the wrong answer." Later she explains that there are certain patterns in the multiple-choice test. "If you're just outright guessing, if a monkey took this test, and you trained him to do just Bs and Cs, he probably would get more right than if he picked As and Ds."

One day, Coach Pingatore picks William up at the learning center, and the two step outside into the brisk Chicago air. William walks with an obvious limp toward Pingatore's late-model car that bears the single word PING on the license plate. Although William is doing his best to improve his test-taking skills, he's afraid that he'll never be able to get it right. At the beginning of the year, when he was showered with letters from every major college in the country, it seemed like all his dreams were about to come true. Now he feels like his whole world is collapsing around him.

"You just don't know the feeling . . . not knowing if you're going to be able to play just because of a test. I mean, as soon as you don't tighten one screw, everything falls apart."

• Something's Missing with Arthur •

He's way behind where I think he should be at this point.
—COACH BEDFORD, discussing Arthur Agee

While William Gates struggles off the basketball court, Arthur Agee struggles on the court. For Arthur— maybe even more than for William—basketball is the most important thing in the world. The hardwood gym floor or the rough concrete playground is the only place where he feels he really belongs, the only place where he can forget the pain and poverty of his family life, the only place where he can just be himself.

"When I played basketball I knew what I wanted to do," he explains. "This is what I want. You know, this is what I want to do for the rest of my life."

That's Arthur's dream—playing basketball for the rest of his life. But the way he plays during his junior year doesn't look too good for the dream. He's undisciplined and out-of-control. Coach Luther Bedford expresses his frustration with Arthur. "He's way behind where I think he should be at this point. I've had a few guys come through from college. 'Ooh, I like that kid. He's quick, he's fast . . .' But something's missing with Arthur."

For a game against rival Crane High School, Arthur's mother and sister come to cheer him on, with Tomika's baby, Jazz, sleeping on Mrs. Agee's lap. Shannon comes, too, dancing in the stands like it's one big party.

Shannon played on the basketball team for a while, but Coach Bedford had to cut him.

"He was a little more raw than Arthur is," Bedford explains with a small laugh. "I couldn't handle two guys like that, so I tried the lesser of two evils. And that was Arthur."

Early in the game, Arthur takes a reckless shot and the defender strips the ball away and passes it down-court for an easy lay-up, with Arthur chasing behind. He grabs the ball after it drops through the basket and pounds it in frustration. Playing carelessly, Arthur gets into foul trouble and spends most of the game on the bench. He isn't the only problem—the whole Marshall squad looks disorganized and out of sync. Coach Bedford is usually pretty calm, but he explodes in the team huddle. "You're just in a hurry to do nothing, cause that's exactly what you're doing—nothing!"

Marshall continues to play poorly, but Crane isn't much better and the score remains close into the fourth quarter. Searching for a spark, Coach Bedford sends Arthur back into the game. At first, it looks like a good move as Arthur takes an outlet pass and drives the length of the court for a quick basket. But in the final minutes, Arthur drives hard toward the hoop and gets called for charging. He fouls out of the game and walks in disappointment back to the bench as Marshall takes another loss.

Even in defeat, Arthur's mother sticks up for her son. "Been some bad calls all day," she says.

"Amen!" Tomika agrees.

Bad calls or not, Marshall's record drops to six wins and fifteen losses. It's their worst record in twenty years.

Arthur has a bad season in school, as well. Unlike William, he never really got enthusiastic about school—not at St. Joseph's, not at Marshall. In a Spanish class, Arthur sits chewing bubble gum and reading the sports pages, completely ignoring the lesson. He's more interested in what Isiah and the Detroit Pistons have been doing than he is in Spanish vocabulary.

"El caballo," says the teacher, pronouncing the Spanish words for "the horse."

"El caballo," the students repeat. Or at least some students repeat it; Arthur is not the only one who's not paying attention.

"La vaca," says the teacher, pronouncing the Spanish words for "the cow."

"La vaca," the students repeat.

Now the teacher approaches Arthur directly, handing him a book and then asking him in Spanish if he has the book. "Arthur, tienes tu el libro? Tienes tu el libro?"

Arthur looks up from the sports pages and blows a big pink bubble with his gum. It's obvious that he has absolutely no idea what the teacher's talking about and he doesn't care. "What I say?" he asks.

"Okay," the teacher says patiently, "how do you say 'yes'?"

Arthur makes a funny face. "Yoi." Some of the students laugh. There is no such word in Spanish, and it's hard to believe that Arthur doesn't know the simple word for "yes." He probably could answer the question, but now he's just goofing around. He likes to make his classmates laugh.

"How do you say 'yes' in Spanish?" the teacher

repeats, a little less patiently than before. "Sí. Look up on the board."

Coach Bedford is just as disappointed in Arthur's academic performance as he is in his basketball performance. And he knows that the academics are more important for Arthur's life. He has seen too many young men just like Arthur.

"He's a pretty smart kid," Bedford says, "but he does just enough to pass. Most of them that have come through here and had that type of attitude end up in the streets talking about how they used to play for Marshall, and if they'd gone to class they could've gone to any school they wanted to."

Coach Bedford's gravelly voice is weary and matter-of-fact. "This is just somebody standing on a street corner talking. You know, trying to find a job that can't find a job. That kind of thing. And this is where he's headed really."

• My Next Year Is Now •

I've seen athletes who have come back from surgery where they worried about the injury. When this happens they may never be the player they were.

—COACH GENE PINGATORE

William enters Coach Pingatore's office and sits in the chair in front of the coach's desk—the same chair where he sat to discuss the ACT results. But now they have another important subject to discuss.

"How's your knee?" Pingatore asks.

"Pretty good," William replies.

"Easiest thing right now would be for you not to play and wait till next year. What do you want to do?" Coach Pingatore speaks quickly and casually. He wants to leave the choice up to William, but it's pretty obvious what he hopes William will decide.

William raises his eyebrows as if it's a very strange question. "And wait till next year?"

"Right."

"No." say William firmly, shaking his head for emphasis.

"Think you're ready?" Pingatore asks.

William smiles confidently. "My next year is now."

William's first start is the final home game of the regular season. As the national anthem plays before the game, he stands thoughtfully with his teammates, his knee sheathed in a padded brace, his eyes half-closed, gazing down at the floor. For a moment he looks upward at the scoreboard. There it is, his name and number back where they belong: 22 Gates.

When the game begins, William seems tentative and cautious. He scrambles for a loose ball with a group of players, but he's afraid to hit the floor hard and gives up the ball rather than fight for it. On the sidelines, Coach Pingatore turns away in frustration. This isn't the William Gates he remembers.

Up in the stands, Curtis Gates sits between his mother and William's girlfriend, Catherine. Curtis analyzes every move that his younger brother makes with the intense eye of an experienced player. When William passes off instead of taking the open shot, Curtis turns to his mother in frustration. "William should have shot it," he says.

Mrs. Gates doesn't say anything. She just watches William nervously, hoping that he'll be all right.

As William gets into the flow of the game, he takes an open jump shot from the left side. Swish! But that's not enough for Curtis. "He's got to do that the whole game," he tells Catherine. "He only does it when they need it."

Catherine doesn't say anything either.

Despite William's mediocre performance, the Chargers roll over their opponent easily. But Curtis isn't concerned about the win. He doesn't like the way William is playing. As he puts on his leather jacket to leave the stands, he tells a friend, "If he don't do something out here on the court, man—he ain't shown me nothin' yet."

William knows that Curtis expects a lot of him, and he doesn't like it. "It was like my injury was making him look bad," he says later. "I always felt that Curtis should not be living his dream through me."

Coach Pingatore expects a lot of William, too. After the players have dressed, the coach has a few tough words for his star player in the corner of the locker room. "You've gotta come out and start playing hard all the time," Pingatore tells him. "Otherwise you're just another player. You follow me?"

William stands in his Chicago Bulls jacket and Michigan Wolverines baseball cap, nodding seriously.

"Just remember the way we talked," Pingatore continues, holding a cold Coke can in his hand. "Okay? As long as you're physically able. If you're not then you shouldn't be playing at all." As he says the last words, Pingatore shrugs and gestures quickly with his hands as if it's all very simple. But for William, it's not simple at all. He wants to play so desperately that it's hard for him to judge whether he's physically able.

After his conversation with the coach, William sits in a quiet corner of the locker room and answers questions from a few sports reporters. In the world of Chicago area high school basketball, the return of William Gates is news. "I was so nervous about the start tonight," he admits. "I'm glad it's over with. Now I can just get into the flow better."

With William back in the line-up, St. Joseph's makes it to the sectional play-offs. In the final minutes of a game against Proviso East, William is fouled and goes to the free throw line. Always a clutch free-throw shooter, he follows the same routine every time he steps to the line. He dribbles the ball three times, lets out a deep breath, and shoots. Swish! Swish! William makes both free throws to send the Chargers ahead by eight. A few moments later, he makes two more free throws to put the game on ice.

In the sectional finals, St. Joe's looks for revenge against Gordon Tech, the team that knocked them out of the playoffs the year before. The gym seems ready to explode, with the St. Joe's fans driven on by the Charger mascot—a student dressed as a Roman centurion with a fake sword and a red and white mask of make-up. "We are . . . St. Joe's!" they shout. "We are . . . St. Joe's!"

William's whole family watches from the stands— his mother, Curtis, and Catherine with baby Alicia in her arms. William's other brothers and sisters are there, too, including his oldest sister, Peggy, and her husband, Alvin.

Despite the show of family support, William plays poorly. He looks out of sync, and he is obviously bothered by his knee. While a Gordon Tech player shoots free throws, William stands in his regular place along the outside of the key, bending over and fingering his knee through the air-hole in the big, cushioned brace.

During a time-out, Coach Pingatore screams at his team. "You are not working! You understand me! They're working harder than you!"

Pingatore's tirade spurs St. Joe's on, and they pick up the pace, taking a slim one-point lead into the fourth quarter. Under the Gordon Tech basket, William leaps up for a rebound and comes down hard, collapsing to the floor and holding his knee in pain. Up in the stands, Curtis can barely stand to watch. Coach Pingatore can't watch either. He turns away as William limps off the floor. While the team doctor examines William's knee on the sideline, Gordon Tech surges ahead, taking a three-point lead with less than three and a half minutes left in the game.

With the doctor's okay, Coach Pingatore sends William back onto the floor. The Chargers close the gap to one point and steal the ball under the Tech basket in the final seconds of the game. William takes the pass, dribbles hard into the front court, and calls time out. On the sidelines, over the steady roar of the crowd, Coach Pingatore outlines a play. It doesn't take a genius to guess that the Chargers want to get the ball to William for an open shot.

After the inbounds pass, Gordon Tech plays tough defense, forcing the Chargers away from the basket, almost out to the half-court line. As the seconds tick away, one of the Chargers fires a long cross-court pass to William in the right corner. He takes a couple of quick dribbles left and a couple to the right, trying to get free of his man, but the defender hangs tough. So William fires a gutsy, eighteen-foot jump shot with the defender in his face. The ball doesn't fall, but he draws a foul. The Charger fans shake the gym, driven on by the Roman centurion and his sword.

With six seconds left in the game, William Gates steps to the line to shoot two free throws. The score is Gordon Tech 65, St. Joseph's 64. Now the gym rocks with the raucous shouts of Gordon Tech fans hoping to make him miss. William's family watches silently, nervously, as if they're holding their breath.

William cradles the ball in his hands and glances up at the basket. Then he begins his routine. He takes three dribbles, blows out a deep breath, and shoots. His form is a little awkward, a little stiff—as if his knee is bothering him. It's not much, but it's enough. The ball arches through the air and comes down hard on the back of the rim, bouncing out into the key. William takes another deep breath and looks down at the floor. He has missed the chance to win. Now all he can do is tie.

Every eye in the auditorium is on him as he steps to the line again, cradling the ball in his hands. With a glance at the basket he begins the routine one more time. Three dribbles. Blow out a deep breath. Shoot. Like a painful instant replay, the ball arches through the air and lands in the exact same spot on the back of the rim. It bounces high above the key, where a Gordon Tech player grabs the rebound and is immediately fouled. As the players shuffle to the other end of the court for another set of free throws, William looks up at the scoreboard and pounds his fist in frustration. Then he bends over and hangs his head toward the ground.

A few seconds later, the buzzer sounds and the Gordon Tech fans pour onto the floor, celebrating another big victory over St. Joe's. They hoist the players onto their shoulders and lift the sectional championship plaque high above their heads. They're on the way to the supersectionals and maybe another trip to Champaign.

William and the Chargers aren't going anywhere except the locker room. They leave the floor as quickly as possible, their heads hanging down as if they don't even want to see the path ahead. Up in the stands, the St. Joseph fans file out just as silently. William's family looks stunned. Mrs. Gates has seen a lot of bad times in her life, but she knows that this is one of the worst times William has ever had to face. She can barely hold back the tears.

William's brother-in-law, Alvin, has a different response. He's disgusted. "He shouldn't have been out there," he says firmly. "He shouldn't have been playing. I'm very disappointed."

Alvin is well-dressed in a red sweater over a red turtleneck. Red is St. Joseph's school color, but right now Alvin isn't too pleased with St. Joseph's High School. Although he's only a little older than Curtis, he speaks with the confidence of a man who has had some success in the world—not the basketball world, but the real world. "I'm disappointed in the system," he continues. "He shouldn't have been out there playing. His knee came out of place a couple of times it looked like. You know, I mean if winning's that important, you need to reevaluate the program."

Curtis doesn't see it that way at all. "That ain't no excuse," he says bluntly. "He got out there, so as far as I'm concerned there wasn't nothing wrong with him. If he was hurt, he shouldn't have gotten out there."

William's family waits outside the locker room like a group of mourners gathered at a wake. When William finally emerges, he wraps his arms around his mother and lays his head on her shoulder, letting the tears flow freely. Catherine and baby Alicia hug him too, trying to comfort him. Peggy and Curtis's wife, Beatrice, stand close by, as if they would like to throw their arms around him, too, while Curtis watches the scene from outside the circle, not quite knowing what to do. Alvin just turns and walks away in disgust—not at William, but at the system that encouraged him to play with a bad knee.

As William and his family leave the gym, the St. Joseph's mascot stands alone in the stands, staring off into space from behind his mask of red and white make-up. He has taken off his costume and dropped his sword to the ground. For this year, at least, the battle is over.

• One More Time •

The only thing on my mind is getting downstate. I want to be able to go all out the whole year. No setbacks, no nothing.

—WILLIAM GATES

Shortly after the loss to Gordon Tech, William's brother-in-law, Alvin, takes him to see Dr. Hefferon, the team doctor for the Chicago Bulls. Dr. Hefferon examines William's knee and looks over the X-rays. Then, with Alvin listening carefully from a chair in the corner of the examining room, he explains the situation.

"There's two possible problems you could have," Dr. Hefferon begins. "You might have healed, say, 80 percent of that cartilage and still have a small residual tear. What you need to do is to get your knee arthroscoped again."

William grimaces at the thought of more surgery, but he knows his knee isn't right, so he agrees to try it again. In the hospital, as a medical assistant prepares his leg for the surgery, William wonders if he made a mistake trying to come back and play during his junior year. "A lot of people say I shouldn't have played, shouldn't have come back at all. Coach kept saying it's really up to me. If you leave it up to me, I'm going to go back out there on the court."

Once again, William goes through all the discomfort of arthroscopic surgery—the IV in his arm, the shots and anesthesia, the incisions in his knee. As the patient lies unconscious on the operating table, Dr. Hefferon probes William's knee with the arthroscope and watches the images on the video screen. Just as he suspected, a part of William's cartilage—called the medial meniscus—never healed completely. Rather than trying to repair the cartilage, he simply removes the damaged part.

"We're gonna remove this portion of the cartilage here," Dr. Hefferon explains behind his operating mask, probing the white tissue with the arthroscope. "He'll have a higher incidence of arthritis as he gets older, but in terms of his basketball career, he has a good chance of performing fine."

Carefully watching the image on the video screen, the surgeon snips away at the damaged cartilage, pulls it out of William's knee through the arthroscope, and lays it on a piece of surgical gauze. "Here's the medial meniscus," he announces. It looks like a half-moon of hard, white gelatin.

"Wow!" someone exclaims. "It's a big piece!" A nurse picks up the tissue with a gloved hand and drops it into a plastic container.

After the surgery, William lays in the recovery room. The anesthesia has worn off, and he is surprisingly alert. He feels optimistic, already looking forward to the next season. "The only thing on my mind," he says, "is getting downstate, just making it down there. I want to be able to go all out the whole year. No setbacks, no nothing." William smiles broadly as he thinks about how good it's going to be to play on a solid knee. "At least Coach won't have to say, 'William, you didn't play hard this game.' 'Cause when I step on that floor, I'm going to be all business and that's it."

Once again William begins the hard grind of physical therapy. But this time, instead of the local YMCA, he works out at the Baxter Clinic, a fancy, high-tech facility used by many of Chicago's professional athletes. The Baxter Clinic offers the latest training equipment and the best physical therapists to supervise his workouts. Both of William's surgeries and his rehabilitation programs have been paid for by St. Joseph's medical insurance plan, so William doesn't have to worry about money. He just has to concentrate on regaining strength and motion in his knee.

After a hard workout, William sits with his leg stretched out on a training table, icing his knee and talking with his physical therapist.

"Don't expect to be playing in a game the first day back," the therapist cautions him.

William nods and grins. "My mother put a big restriction on the pick-up games," he says, drawing a laugh from the therapist. "She says these are her knees now."

One day, William goes to visit his father, Willie Crawford. Mr. Crawford left the family when William was just a baby, and William hasn't seen the older man for three years. William doesn't think much about his father anymore. "It just never popped into my mind," he says. But when Mr. Crawford invited him to come and see his auto repair shop, William decided to go ahead and visit him.

It's spring, and the air is mild with a hint of blue sky peeking from behind the clouds. William wears his Bulls jacket and a baseball cap. He is still walking with a limp.

Mr. Crawford looks a lot like William—or William looks a lot like Mr. Crawford. The same strong features;

the same powerful, solid build. But the similarity is only on the surface, in the way they look. As people, they don't have any real connection at all. Now Mr. Crawford is trying to make some sort of contact with his son. He has a car that he's been fixing up for William, but it isn't quite ready yet.

"The car that I was going to give you, I didn't finish it up yet," Mr. Crawford says when William steps into the small office of his auto shop. "I got some more to do to it yet."

William follows his father outside to take a look at the car. It's a white Oldsmobile Cutlass—a big, old car that definitely needs some more work. William slips into the driver's seat and checks it out. It doesn't look so hot on the inside; the steering wheel is gone and half of the electrical system hangs down from the dashboard. William doesn't show much excitement or emotion. He is suspicious about his father's reasons for suddenly inviting him to visit and offering him a gift.

"I think he's like, 'Oh, he must really be able to play some basketball.' And he thinks now he sees something at the end for himself." William doesn't have a lot of respect for his father since Mr. Crawford abandoned the family. As far as William is concerned, he isn't much of a father at all. "I remember one time he tried to whup me," William explains. "But I wouldn't let him. I said, 'You may be my Dad biologically, but as far as being there—you're not.'"

After looking at the car, William and Mr. Crawford head back into the office of the auto shop. Despite his anger at his father over the past, William can't help being a little curious about him. Along with his regular business as an auto mechanic, Mr. Crawford works in the evenings as a blues singer. But William has never heard him.

"You say you'd like to come to my next show that I do?" Mr. Crawford asks.

"Yeah," William says with a small smile, "come out and finally get a chance to see you sing."

Mr. Crawford nods. "Okay. Well what I'll have to do . . . I don't have my schedule right this minute, but I'll have to get that, and I'll let you know." William doesn't really expect he'll ever get the schedule—like the car, which his dad never delivers on.

Back at Cabrini Green, William sits in the kitchen and plays with his daughter Alicia, snuggling her close. "They say you're my only friend," he says. "All right? Gimme five." He holds up his hand, and Alicia slaps him a rock-solid baby five. Catherine watches happily, enjoying the warm relationship between William and Alicia.

"I always knew that I was gonna be a better Dad than he was," William says seriously. "I wouldn't just leave her like that. If Alicia has a problem, then I have a problem."

Suddenly Alicia launches into a long lecture in baby talk. It doesn't make much sense, but she's definitely trying to say something very important. William listens and laughs. "She means whatever she said."

• Turned Around •

He can just look at my life and say here's a good example of what not to do.

—MR. AGEE, after his release from jail

In the summer of 1990, a year after he walked out on them, Mr. Agee returns to his family. During the time he was away, he spent seven months in jail for burglary and overcame an addiction to crack cocaine—a deadly form of the drug that's easy to buy on the city streets. Now he hopes to make up for the mistakes of the past and help his family toward a new and better future.

Like many people who have hit bottom, Mr. Agee turned to God for help. "While I was incarcerated," he explains, "I just asked God, 'Show me a different way. Give me a new life. Take the taste of drugs and evil way of thinking away from me.' I asked the Lord to forgive me for what I did—the times that I mistreated my wife, beat her physically, you know. I just hope this be a lesson to my children to see me turn my life over to the Lord."

On a Sunday morning, Mr. and Mrs. Agee walk with their family to church on the city's South Side. Mrs. Agee looks pretty in a royal blue dress and dangling earrings, but the real star is her granddaughter, Jazz, cradled in her arms in a frilly white dress with red bows in her hair. Mr. Agee walks beside his wife in a light blue shirt and dark blue tie. He still looks skinny, but there's a new strength and purpose in his steps. The three children follow behind: Tomika, dressed in a stylish black-and-white checked dress; Arthur, in a white shirt and long, thin black tie; and Joseph—the only Agee man who gets to go to church without a tie.

As they turn the corner toward the small brick building, the Agees look like a model family from the pages of a magazine. It's hard to believe that this is the same family that was torn apart by drugs and physical abuse. But although they look healthy and happy on the outside, the pain is still there on the inside.

The church is simply decorated with a table for the Bible, a wooden lectern for the preacher, and an organ in the corner. Twenty or thirty people sit on the straight-backed wooden benches at the beginning of the service. The preacher is a heavy-set woman with a kindly, open face. She wears a flowing robe and speaks with a rolling, musical rhythm that produces nods and smiles and shouts of agreement from her congregation.

"Men might fail you, but Jesus never fails—Praise God! If you haven't tried him, try him. You know sometime you look for friends and they're not there. But Jesus is always there. Even in the midnight hour, he's there." Mr. Agee smiles and nods in his seat. He knows about the midnight hour. "Glory to God. Hallelujah!"

Mr. and Mrs. Agee come forward with Jazz for a special blessing. They kneel before the preacher and bow their heads. Arthur sits stiffly in the bench behind them, watching without emotion. It's obvious that he still has doubts about his father.

"Lord, we know you always blessed the family," the preacher begins, holding her open palms over the bowed heads of Mr. and Mrs. Agee. "Glory to God, even in the beginning, Lord, you blessed that first family. Glory to God, we pray right now don't let nothing come between them. Send strength, Lord, glory to God, wherever there's weakness. Please, Lord, let the love prevail."

After the blessing, Mr. Agee sings a song that seems to speak directly from his personal experience. He has a beautiful singing voice—rich and melodious. "I've had my good days. I've seen some bad days. I've had my ups and downs. And, Lord, I've been turned around. . . ." The way he holds the microphone comfortably in his hand, with the organ playing quietly behind him, it's obvious that Mr. Agee has done some singing in his life. "I want to thank you, Lord, for protecting my family—I just want to say thank you, Lord."

The congregation sways in their seats, nodding in appreciation of Mr. Agee's beautiful voice—and his commitment to changing his way of life. Mrs. Agee breaks into a broad, happy smile. She wants to believe that her husband has really changed. She wants to love him again. But Arthur is still angry. He stares straight ahead without expression.

"I want to thank you, Lord, for protecting my family," Mr. Agee sings again. "I just want to say thank you, Lord. Lord, I won't complain. You washed my tears away . . ."

Suddenly Arthur has had enough. He jumps out of his seat, walks back down the aisle, and leaves the church with his father still singing in front of the congregation.

Back in the Agee home, Arthur expresses his feelings. He's changed out of his church clothes into a T-shirt and backwards baseball cap with an orange basketball and the number eleven painted across the back.

"When I was little, you know, he had let me down. People used to come up to me and say, 'Your father's a drug addict. Your father's on drugs,' and stuff. I used to be like, 'Yeah, okay.' You know, I used to take so much, that [Bo] started realizing what is he doing. 'Cause I remember sometimes he used to try to go to church while he was still on drugs."

Mr. Agee sits in the living room, his shirt off, playing happily with Jazz. Of course, Jazz is just a baby, and she doesn't have any bad memories of her grandfather. Arthur is a different story, and Mr. Agee realizes it's going to take some time to patch up their relationship. "The closeness was not there at first when I come back home," he admits, "and then Arthur, he was watching me—what move would I make now. Am I just being like this since I just come back, or am I going to break bad again?"

That summer, Arthur and Shannon attend summer school together for the second year in a row. They're placed in an English class that includes freshmen, sophomores, and juniors. It's not an ideal situation, but it's the best they can do at Marshall. "The basic problem here is that we were strapped for money," explains the teacher, Mr. Kelly, "and we only had one English class available to our students. Hopefully, you can touch a nerve with some of them. Like a spirited discussion on a controversial topic."

One day, he picks a topic that's sure to get a spirited response from any group of teenagers. "When you're out on a date," he asks, "do you have to have sex?"

The whole class explodes with a chorus of shouted answers. Mr. Kelly has definitely touched a nerve, but he can't hear anything they're saying because they're all shouting at once. "Quiet down a minute here!" he demands.

Arthur and Shannon goof around and slap each other five over something that Arthur says amid the confusion. Mr. Kelly wants Arthur to say it for the whole class. "Restate your question," he tells him.

Arthur looks off to the side, as if the answer is written on the blackboard. "What'd I say?" he asks, knowing it'll get laughs. The whole class cracks up, but Mr. Kelly keeps on trying.

Arthur keeps trying, too, in his own way. He goofs around and he doesn't pay much attention, but at least he keeps coming to class. Shannon is a different story. "Shannon didn't really care," Mr. Kelly explains, "so he just stopped coming and he was dropped from the roll."

Even if Arthur passes summer school, he might not graduate with his class. As other private schools would, St. Joseph's refuses to send his records to Marshall until the Agees pay the money they owe. Along with teaching English, Mr. Kelly serves as the school registrar, an official in charge of records. He called St. Joseph's to see if he could get Arthur's records, but they declined. "The lady explained to me that he owed $1,800. So I felt like they have a school policy, and there's nothing I can do about that."

During the summer Arthur's parents decide that they had better do something about it. They go out to St. Joseph's and meet with the school's Director of Finances, Michael J. O'Brien. Arthur isn't with them, but Mr. Agee holds Jazz on his lap as they discuss a monthly payment plan.

"About how much can you afford?" asks Mr. O'Brien, a pudgy, red-faced man wearing an open-collared plaid shirt. He seems uncomfortable about this interview. The sign outside his office indicates that he accepts Visa and MasterCard, but he knows the Agees can't pay with credit cards.

"Okay," Mr. Agee replies nervously "we're looking at eighteen . . ."

"Thirteen, ten."

Mr. Agee's eyes light up. "Oh! Thirteen, ten?" He thinks that maybe the total is really $1,310, five hundred dollars less than he expected. But Mr. O'Brien repeats the whole total: $1,813.10.

"Oh," Mr. Agee says, a little disappointed. "And to total that out from here to June, his graduation date . . ."

Mr. O'Brien punches the number into his desktop calculator. "We're looking at somewhere around $181.30 per month."

Mr. Agee nods. It's a lot of money, money they can't afford. But he is determined to do what's right for Arthur. Now he asks the real question, cautiously, carefully. "Is there any possible way that his—I don't know, I'm just asking—could his credits be released, too?"

Mr. O'Brien nods. "I will get a promissory agreement drawn up, okay? And as long as you show me good faith after the first two months, I'll release them. That would be end of September. And I'll send them to Marshall."

The tension in the room evaporates, and Mr. and Mrs. Agee break into big smiles. "Okay, then," Mrs. Agee says, "that will be fine with us. And I really appreciate this."

"How is Arthur doing anyway?" Mr. O'Brien asks pleasantly.

"Pretty good, you know," Mrs. Agee replies. "I can't really complain about him. Wish he could have stayed here, though."

Mr. O'Brien shrugs and tries to make light of the situation. "Well, you know, things happen you know . . ."

"Things happen you know," Mrs. Agee agrees. "It's part of life."

Mr. Agee interrupts the small talk, his voice serious and emotional, as though he's about to cry. "I can't let him down no more."

Now Mr. O'Brien is really uncomfortable. He's not used to having emotional real-life scenes in his office. "Okay, good. Okay, I hope we can work something out."

"I'd like to thank you-ou." Mr. Agee almost sings the words as he reaches across the room to shake hands with the other man.

"No problem."

"Thank God for you. For what you've done for us."

Suddenly even Mr. O'Brien is touched by Mr. Agee's genuine concern for his son. "No problem," he says again, with more feeling than before. "I understand that, and that's what we're here for—to try and help people."

The Agees get up to leave, and Mr. O'Brien tries to usher them out the door. But Mr. Agee steps back to throw his arms around the school official and gives him a warm embrace, causing Mr. O'Brien's red face to turn even redder with embarrassment. Finally, the Agees walk out through the clean hallways of St. Joseph's High School and head back to their world on the west side of Chicago.

As Mr. Agee guides their old car through the streets of Garfield Park, he reflects on his own mistakes and how he has hurt Arthur. "I think about it—had I not been on drugs when Arthur went to St. Joe's—just how good it would have been for him." Keeping his hands on the wheel, he glances out the open window at a street corner where a group of men are hanging out in the shadow of a dark brick apartment building. "Here's one of the corners . . . I used to come up here and cop all the time." "Cop" is slang for buying drugs.

Now the car passes another corner where a drug dealer is standing right in the street, holding up a small white packet for sale. Behind him a group of children play in a tot lot. "I threw away a lot of money on these corners, boy," Mr. Agee admits. "Almost threw my life right along with it."

Finally Mr. Agee pulls over to the curb in front of his home. He leans back for a moment and thinks about Arthur and the temptations his son faces in this neighborhood. "He can just look at my life and say here's a good example of what not to do." Mr. Agee smiles, thankful that Arthur is stronger than he is. "If he had my ways, I would be shakin' in my shoes right now."

• Summer Camp •

c h a p t e r   1 7

*It's already become a meat market, but I try to do my
job and serve professional meat.*

—BOB GIBBONS, independent college scout

That summer, Arthur and Shannon work at Pizza Hut
for $3.35 an hour. The two friends clown around in the
kitchen, dancing to the sounds of a boom box and slicing a pizza together as they count out loud with every
chop of the big knife: "One, two, three, four." When the
pizza is ready, Arthur carries it out to the customers. He
puts on a big grin, waltzes gracefully across the room,
and lays the pizza on the table with a flourish. "How
y'all doin' today?"

When their shift is over, they head over to the playground to shoot some hoops. The Chicago summer days
are long, and there's plenty of time to practice before dark.

One day Arthur, Shannon, and another friend check
out the latest styles at a local sports clothing store.
Shannon has got his eye on a Georgetown coat with a
pocket on the side. Arthur likes it, too, but he decides to
go with a purple Michael Jordan sweatshirt and match-
ing sweatpants. He brings the clothing up to the counter
and asks the clerk, "How much?"

"Seventy bucks, even," the clerk replies. "No tax." At
this store in the heart of the ghetto, they do business a
little differently than they do it out in the suburbs.

96
Paul Robert Walker

Arthur hands the clerk the money and walks out with his new sweat suit. Seventy dollars is a lot of money for a boy who only works part-time at $3.35 an hour, but Arthur isn't spending his own money. "Some of the drug pushers in the neighborhood give us money to tell us 'go shop' and 'go get you something,'" Shannon explains. "They're thinking we play basketball and they can give us stuff and keep our career going. So that's how we really keep up with the styles."

Almost a thousand miles away, William Gates has a very different summer experience. He is invited to the prestigious Nike All-American Camp at Princeton University in New Jersey. On the first day, basketball announcer Dick Vitale gives the players a pep talk. A small balding man in white gym shorts and a red, white and blue shirt, Vitale prances back and forth across the stage, gesturing wildly with his hands and shouting in his famous, booming, overenthusiastic voice:

"While you're sitting here today," he screams, "you should feel like a million dollars! You should feel so special! You are one of a hundred of the best high school players in this country, the United States! My mother— God bless her she's in heaven today—she used to always say to me, 'This is America! You can make something of your life!'"

As the young players listen to Vitale, they have different reactions. Some are impressed; after all, he is a famous sports announcer and they've heard him on television. Others think he's a little crazy, the way he screams and runs around the stage. But they all understand what he's talking about—opportunity. That's the name of the game at the Nike camp. Every major college coach comes to check out the hottest players heading into their final year of high school.

"There's two hundred fifty of us here," says Kevin O'Neill, head coach at Marquette University. "We're doing it to find out who the best players are and try to get them in our program."

Bobby Knight, the famous coach at Indiana University, understands how tough it is to find just the right player for his program. "There aren't many kids at any level, including the NBA, who understand what basketball is all about."

Joey Meyer, head coach at DePaul University, puts a different spin on the situation. "We always say you're going to war. Would you want him behind you covering your flank?"

As the coaches head up into the stands, the players prepare for action down on the gym floor. One of the camp coaches gives them a few pointers. "If you're a player," he says, "someone up there is going to recognize you're a player." Everyone knows that "up there" means up in the stands where the coaches and scouts sit with their little notebooks. "If you're pouting, they're also going to recognize that, and don't tell me they're not going to write it down in that book."

In the early scrimmages, William gets frustrated. His knee feels strong, and he dances around the floor trying to get open for a pass—just the way he does at St. Joseph's. But no one will pass him the ball. They're all too busy trying to score points on their own.

"It's a waste of my time down here," he mutters. "I'm ready to go home. Here I am always trying to play this team ball. The more coaches come around and look, everybody feel they got to do their own little thing here."

Along with the practices and games, the players attend daily classes. It's a long day, and it's tough to sit in the classroom during the summer. But the Nike camp wants to offer the players more than just an opportunity to show off their skills on the court. The camp tries to help prepare them for the reality of big-time college basketball. The camp academic director, Frank Dubois, explains, "We provide them with an experience you can't get anywhere else in that we simulate what it's going to be like to be a student athlete. The statistics on Division I players graduating from college are really frightening." What's frightening is that most players don't graduate.

During one class, a teacher tries to show the players how to manage their time. He lists the number of hours each week they'll have to spend in classes, the number of hours they'll need for studying, and the number of hours they'll spend on basketball. "How many hours do we have up here?" he asks. The numbers add up to a sixty-one-hour work week, much longer than the hours an average person spends on a job. "Let's suppose you're playing big-time college basketball," the teacher continues, "and your team travels . . ." Some of the players aren't paying attention, but William listens carefully. He can picture himself playing big-time basketball.

In another class, the famous film director Spike Lee gives the mostly black players at the camp his perspective on big-time college basketball. "You have to realize that nobody cares about you," he says. "You're black, you're a young male—all you're supposed to do is deal drugs and mug women. The only reason you're here is because you can make their team win. If their team wins, these schools get a lot of money. This whole thing is revolving around money."

Marquette coach Kevin O'Neill doesn't necessarily agree with everything Spike Lee says, but he agrees that money plays an important part in big-time basketball. A winning team fills the seats, generates television revenue, and brings in more contributions to the school. "Recruiting is like any other sales business," he says. "We've got to win to keep our jobs. We've got to fill the arena to keep our jobs, and if we don't, they fire us. Hey, if bankers don't make money, they fire them."

One of O'Neill's assistant coaches is Bo Ellis, a former Marquette star who went on to play in the NBA. Standing with a group of other coaches, Ellis watches the young players walking across campus and admires their powerful physiques. "I tell you what man, you look at some of these young boys' bodies—they got NBA bodies already."

When another coach admits that he's been following one player since sixth grade, Ellis nods his head in understanding. "That's when you want to get on 'em— when they're young—and start writing them before everybody else writes them."

Bob Gibbons is a highly-respected independent scout who sells his services to a variety of colleges. He knows the recruiting business is just that—a business. "It's already become a meat market," he admits, "but I try to do my job and serve professional meat."

As the camp continues, William gets into the flow of the games. One afternoon, with Bob Gibbons watching carefully, he puts on a star performance. He drives down the court, switches directions with a behind-the-back dribble, and nails a jump shot from the free-throw line. Then he nails another jumper from the top of the key.

"What schools do you think are most involved with William right now?" Gibbons asks a fellow scout.

"I would say DePaul, Michigan, Marquette, Indiana."

Gibbons continues to watch as William takes a pass down low, dribbles under the basket and makes a soft turn-around jumper while drawing the foul. "Excellent!" the scout exclaims. High in the stands, Kevin O'Neill of Marquette is watching, too.

When William comes out of the game, his camp coach greets him with a high-five. "Good job! Way to go!"

That night in his dorm room, William bubbles over with excitement as he tells a group of other players about his top-notch performance. "Bob Gibbons done seen me play my best game out here. Turned in sixteen points, twelve assists! Bob Gibbons is over there like this, hmmm . . ." William holds his own appointment book in his hands and pantomimes the scout writing in his little notebook. "Yeah, I was smiling, too, Bob."

The other players laugh in appreciation. Even though they're competing for scholarships, they're all in this together. They understand how good it feels to play your best when the scouts and coaches are watching. The players in the room are all from the Chicago area, and they enjoy each other's company. It's a great adventure, being away from home and checking out life in a college dorm. Maybe the best part of all is when the pizza arrives. They rip open the box and attack the pizza as if they haven't eaten for weeks.

After his great game, William has a whole new attitude toward the camp. "Right now, I'm just feeling good about myself. Since I been down here, I really feel like I am an All-American. When I go home, I'm going to feel unstoppable."

Then the bubble bursts. During a brilliant game, William makes a quick reverse and twists something in his right leg—the same leg where he has had two knee surgeries. He knows immediately that something is very wrong and that camp is over for him. It's a crushing disappointment and William can barely contain his frustration. He limps off the court into one of the exit areas of the big university arena and lies down in agony. Up in the stands, Indiana coach Bobby Knight watches with concern as a doctor examines William's leg.

"Okay, I'm going to pull up on it. Tell me if it hurts more."

"Yeah!" William moans.

"Okay, easy does it now." The doctor slowly moves the leg back to its original position. "It's on the muscle, not on the joint. It's above the joint, okay?"

William nods, but his face is tight with pain. It's only a muscle injury—not a knee injury—but it's bad enough that William cannot compete for the final two days of the camp.

• Sign on the Dotted Line •

As soon as William tells me that he's not looking at any other schools, then I'm not looking at any other players.

—KEVIN O'NEILL,
Marquette University basketball coach

In the Gates family living room, Mrs. Gates holds a letter in her hand and reads while Curtis sprawls on the couch and watches a daytime soap opera. "Don't let your best opportunity get away from you. You can have a great experience at Marquette University. Once you visit our campus, I feel confident that you will know that Marquette is the right place for you. Sincerely, Kevin O'Neill."

Mrs. Gates brings the letter down from her face to reveal a big smile. "I like these. I've been getting like two a week from the school for a couple of months. So it's quite a few." She gestures to a pile of Federal Express mailers on the table. Sending letters by Federal Express costs a lot more money than the regular mail. Marquette is obviously trying to make a strong impression on the Gates family.

Later, Curtis gets up and heads for the local basketball courts, dribbling as he walks through the back streets of Cabrini Green. In a red shirt and gray sweat shorts, he looks even heavier than before, way out of shape from his brilliant playing days. "I had Division I offers," he says, referring to the top level of college basketball. "I had even signed at Marquette, 'cause they thought I was going to make the grades." But he didn't make the grades; that's why he went to a junior college. And even though he's frustrated that he never got a college degree, he still thinks his attitude was right. "The great ballplayers, they care about basketball more than school, and I know they do."

At the Cabrini Green courts, Curtis gets into a game of "Horse" where each player has to make the same shot as the player before him. When a player drives under the basket for a reverse dunk, Curtis tries to do the same. But he can't jump high enough to dunk anymore, and his attempt to lay it in off the backboard bounces off the rim. Curtis mutters something about being out of shape, and stands off to the side to watch another player making an acrobatic dunk. Cabrini Green is full of great ballplayers.

During the fall of William's senior year, Kevin O'Neill, Bo Ellis, and another Marquette coach visit the Gates home to recruit William for their team. Gene Pingatore is also there, along with Curtis and William's brother-in-law, Alvin. This is William's first official home recruiting visit. Three top schools have postponed their visits to see how William does during his senior year at St. Joe's.

The visit begins with a videotape that describes the Marquette basketball program and their history of success. "If you're looking for a progressive college basketball program with experienced leadership and a winning tradition, then the Marquette Warriors are for you."

When the tape is over, Kevin O'Neill sits down in front of William and his mother to make his pitch. He tries to assure them that William matters to Marquette University as a person, not just as a basketball player. "If you don't make the test score that doesn't mean we don't want you, because we still do, that's what I'm telling you. If you tear your knee out again this year, and you can't ever play again, you're going to have your education paid for at Marquette University."

Coach Pingatore interrupts. He's heard hundreds of recruiting pitches before. "I know that the scholarship is one year renewable . . ."

O'Neill nods, but he doesn't miss a beat. "Gene's right about this, but any school worth a salt is gonna give you four years. The bottom line is this: we want to win the national title. Number two: I want to make you the best player I can." O'Neill has a smooth, sincere, and intelligent way of speaking, like a college professor mixed with a traveling salesman. "I want to give you the opportunity to maybe someday be one of those guys who goes out and makes some money in Europe or the NBA. You're one of seven guys we're recruiting right now."

From behind the living room couch, Curtis leans forward and enters the conversation. "You're recruiting seven guys?"

"Seven guys for three spots."

Curtis gestures toward William. "Where's he fit in?"

"Where's he fit in?"

"Yeah."

O'Neill shrugs slightly and lays it on the line. "As soon as William tells me that he's not looking at any other schools, then I'm not looking at any other players."

After the recruiting visit, William decides to visit the Marquette University campus in Milwaukee, Wisconsin, about ninety miles north of Chicago. Bo Ellis shows him around the Bradley Center, the huge stadium where the Marquette Warriors play their home games. Ellis is a tall, powerfully-built black man who is growing the beginnings of a beard. He has been where William wants to go—college star and NBA player. When Bo Ellis talks, William listens.

"This is a great place, and we're getting ready to have it rockin', too. The best is yet to come. A lot of serious ballplayers have been through this building. Junior Bridgeman. Sydney Moncrief. Bob Lanier. Oscar Robertson." Ellis gestures toward the stadium seats, empty and silent now, but full of promise for the coming seasons. "Can you see yourself playing in this place here? Eighteen thousand in it. Big difference from St. Joe's now."

William looks around the Bradley Center, imagining himself playing in front of eighteen thousand screaming fans. He likes the idea—this is definitely big-time basketball. His gaze moves upward toward the ceiling where two championship banners hang as reminders of past glories: NCAA 1977, NIT 1970. These are the two great tournaments of college basketball. The NCAA is the biggest, with the top teams in the country playing for the chance to hang that banner in their arenas. The NIT is a tournament for the best of the rest. And Marquette has won them both.

During William's time at Marquette, Coach O'Neill and his staff do everything possible to make sure he enjoys himself. They put up William and his mother at the Hyatt, a fancy hotel near the campus. "Man, it was nice. They had these balloons all hanging up on the ceiling and everything. They really did it up. I must say. We did it up too . . . room service." William laughs at the thought of all the great food they ordered from room service—paid for by Marquette. "Man!"

Kevin O'Neill not only wants William to enjoy himself, he wants him to imagine what it will be like playing for the Marquette Warriors. He has phony newspapers printed up with headlines like: GATES FIRST M. U. PLAYER TO RECORD TRIPLE-DOUBLE. A triple-double means the player reaches double figures (ten or over) in points, assists, and rebounds or steals. That's the kind of all-around performance Marquette hopes to see from William, and it's the kind of performance that could take William all the way to the NBA.

After his tour of the arena, William and his mother join Coach O'Neill and his staff in a luxury sky box, high above the basketball floor. They play a cassette tape of a phony radio broadcast of William competing for Marquette. "Notre Dame 77, Marquette 76," the announcer begins. "Gates is out high calling for the ball! There are six seconds left. The freshman spins past a defender, slicing to the left of the foul line." William listens intently, enjoying the fantasy. "Three seconds left, Marquette down by one. Gates launches a flying one-hander . . . It is on the way. It is—GOOD! Gates buries a thirteen footer just ahead of the horn and Marquette has defeated Notre Dame!" William breaks into a huge grin, almost as if the game were real.

Across the sky box, Mrs. Gates sits on a couch, listening and smiling, too. She knows that the Marquette staff is trying to influence William. But she appreciates the fact that these people seem to care so much about her son.

As if he can read her thoughts, Coach O'Neill turns to William and drives home his point. "If you think we care about you a lot in recruiting, we're going to do more when you're here. You know that," he says sincerely. "Don't let it get to a point where somebody else comes in and takes a scholarship away. 'Cause it's yours right now if you want the darn thing."

O'Neill pauses for a moment to let it all sink in. "Let us know what you want to do," he says. "Unless you know what you want to do right now."

William tries to control the smile on his face, but he doesn't quite succeed. O'Neill laughs good-naturedly. "He knows but he won't say."

When William returns to St. Joseph's after his trip to Marquette, he meets with Coach Pingatore in his office. He tells the coach that he wants to go to Marquette, and Pingatore expresses some doubts. "That's fine," he says, but his tone of voice suggests that maybe it isn't fine. "Now obviously if you wait, you'll have all the other schools that were on you before, like Kansas and Indiana, North Carolina State." Although he doesn't say it, Coach Pingatore knows that oftentimes a player will be inclined to sign immediately following a successful recruiting visit. He thinks William should consider other schools before making a decision.

"It's all right," William says firmly, "I discussed it with my . . ."

Coach Pingatore interrupts him in mid-sentence. "I think you should take a few days. Because you just came back, you understand?"

But William has made up his mind. A few days later, at the home of his sister Peggy and her husband, Alvin, he signs an official letter of intent, promising to attend Marquette University. He can't officially accept the scholarship until he scores an eighteen on his ACT, but Marquette and William are both assuming that he'll get the score he needs.

Peggy has bought alcohol-free champagne to celebrate the big event, and William pops the cork like an expert. As Alvin pours the champagne into glasses, William signs the letter. "Is there any cash with this?" he asks, jokingly.

"It's in the mail," says Alvin, and they share a laugh. They raise their champagne glasses, as Alvin proposes a toast. "To four years of excellence!"

"Here! Here!"

• Happy Birthday, Arthur •

It's his eighteenth birthday, he lived, and to get to see eighteen—that's good!

—Mrs. Sheila Agee

While William makes plans to attend Marquette University, Arthur faces an uncertain future. Early in his senior year, his records from St. Joseph's finally arrive at Marshall, and Arthur meets with his counselor, Mrs. Mitchell, to discuss his credits.

"If you pass all of the classes you are presently taking, you can graduate in summer school," Mrs. Mitchell tells him. "Okay?"

Arthur nods, but he isn't too happy about it. Another year of summer school!

"Have you taken the ACT?" the counselor asks. Arthur shakes his head. "When do you plan to take it?"

Arthur shrugs and mumbles, "Sometime soon."

Mrs. Mitchell is not pleased with Arthur's vague attitude. This is the beginning of his senior year, and most students who intend to go to college take the ACT during their junior year. "What institution are you planning on going to?" she asks. "Have you decided that?"

"I was thinking about going to Alabama."

"But you need to take Algebra Trig. OK? Do you plan to take that?"

Arthur squirms in his seat and manages an embarrassed smile. "I don't know."

Now Mrs. Mitchell is getting annoyed. Advanced algebra and trigonometry are required for four-year colleges like Alabama. "You don't know! So you're just getting by again."

Arthur squirms some more. He can't even look the counselor in the face. "Nah, you ain't got to say that."

"But you are," Mrs. Mitchell insists. "You've been barely getting by all along. Now you're going to have to do better than that if you want to go to Alabama or any other school. You're going to have to do more than just get by."

Arthur leaves the counselor's office and expresses his frustration outside in the hallway. He blames his troubles on St. Joe's, but fails to see his own role in his problems there. "St. Joe just messed everything up. I shouldn't have even went there. Thought I had more credits than this." He holds the transcript in his hand and shakes the paper in frustration. His parents have had to make expensive monthly payments in order to get these records, and now they didn't even turn out to help him as much as he had hoped. Arthur feels a lot of anger about the way he's been treated by St. Joseph's, but he shows an impressive inner strength. "That all right though," he says firmly. "I'm still going to make it." Then he climbs the staircase and goes to class.

In October, Arthur celebrates his eighteenth birthday. His mother makes him a special birthday dinner and a special cake. For Mrs. Agee, it's a happy day, a time to be thankful for the good things in life after all the sorrow of the past. "I want to show him how much we appreciate him and love him and care for him. Everything you can imagine was going wrong with this family, but now everybody's together." With the dinner cooking on the stove, she spreads German chocolate frosting on a homemade cake. "It's his favorite cake. He's a great kid. And some kids don't even live to get this age, you know," she says seriously, thinking about the violence of the inner city streets. "That's another thing to be proud about. It's his eighteenth birthday, he lived, and to get to see eighteen—that's good!"

Mr. Agee is also proud of Arthur. With the family and Arthur's friends gathered around, he stands in the living room and holds the birthday cake on a plate, the eighteen candles already burning. "I want to tell you that I love you very much," he says. "I'm very proud of you. Seems like I was eighteen just yesterday. Here. Happy Birthday. I love you." Mr. Agee holds out the birthday cake, and Arthur takes it in his own hands, accepting a kiss from his father with a smile. Today, at least, they seem to have patched up their differences. As everyone sings happy birthday to him, Arthur sits down with the cake on his lap and casually blows out the candles.

Unfortunately, the warm glow of good feelings doesn't last for long in the Agee home. Two months after his eighteenth birthday, Arthur is cut off from Public Aid, putting added financial pressure on the family. Once again, Mrs. Agee is furious at the system. Even though Arthur is eighteen years old, he's still a full-time high school student.

"They feel like when they get eighteen, most black kids drop out," Mrs. Agee explains. "So that means that the child is just thrown out there. I was getting $368, now I get $268. And that's it. And this is to take care of me from one month to the next. Now can you imagine a person living on that? Do you wonder sometimes how am I living? Or how do my children survive?"

Mrs. Agee is a warm, loving woman, but she can barely control her fury at the fact that her son has been abandoned by the system. "It's enough to make people really want to go out there and just lash out and hurt somebody."

While Mrs. Agee tells her story, Arthur plays with baby Jazz, tickling her and rolling her around. Later he sits in his room, cleaning his basketball shoes and listening to an angry rap song about blacks who try to live in the white world. "No matter how much you want to switch," the song says, "here's what they think about you: Fried chicken and biscuit eating monkey, baboon, big-thighed, fast-running, high-jumping, spear-chucking, 360-degree basketball dunking, pit, spade—moron!"

In wraparound shades, Arthur nods his head with the rhythm and keeps on cleaning his shoes.

• Upset! •

William Gates stinks.

—COACH PINGATORE, fall 1990

After the sky-high excitement of being recruited by Marquette University, William has to come down to earth and prepare for his senior season at St. Joseph's High School. At first it seems like a long, hard fall. In a preseason league, William looks awkward and out of sync, like he's not really focusing on the game. He loses the ball on the dribble and then makes a half-hearted effort to get it back, only to lose it again.

From the sidelines, Coach Pingatore and his assistant, Dennis Doyle, watch the preseason action. They don't like what they see.

"William Gates stinks," says Pingatore bluntly. "You got that—he stinks."

Coach Doyle is a little more subtle in his explanation of William's problems. "He doesn't play with confidence like he did before he was injured. I don't believe the other players have complete confidence in William. They were in awe of William when he was a sophomore. They're not in awe of him anymore."

William knows that he's struggling, that he has lost something he had before his injury. "Sophomore year, I was just carefree," he remembers. "If it could be done, I was gonna do it. I wish I could get that attitude back."

One day William visits his grammar school gym. It's a small, old gymnasium—tiny compared to St. Joseph's gym and microscopic compared to the huge arena at Marquette. But this is where he got his start. This is where it all began. William steps to the free throw line, dribbles the ball three times, and takes a good look at the basket. Then he closes his eyes and concentrates, trying to visualize the ball going through the hoop. With his eyes still closed, he sets and shoots. Swish! Nothing but net.

As the official season begins, Coach Pingatore is still unhappy with William's performance. In one practice, the team runs a fast-break drill, working on getting the ball downcourt as quickly as possible. William leads the break, dribbling hard down the right side. But instead of driving through an opening in the defense, he dishes it off to a teammate with a casual shovel pass that just misses the mark. The teammate can't reach it, and the whole play falls apart.

"Hold up!" Pingatore shouts. "That's crap! Why did you have to do something unnecessarily? If you would have kept it over here, William . . ." In the middle of the lecture, William turns away and walks upcourt. "Look at me!" the coach demands. "If you'd have kept it over here, why, you could've gone all the way. What is that crap—the shovel pass?"

Coach Pingatore has always shouted at his players. That's nothing new. It's part of his personality, and Pingatore's personality and basketball knowledge have produced many successful teams. Earlier in his high school career, William accepted the shouting and tough discipline as the price he had to pay to be a great player.

But now, in his senior year, he's getting a little tired of it. He longs for the free-wheeling exhilaration of playing basketball for the pure joy of the game. "There's never any point in our school where we play outright."

Coach Pingatore demands total concentration on the court and off. During the season, as the players board the bus for an away game, their faces are as somber as the cold, gray Chicago winter. "Remember," Pingatore tells the team as they settle into their seats, "think about the ball game on the way to the game." The bus pulls away from the school with the players sitting stiffly and silently. Maybe they're thinking about the game, maybe they're not. But no one says a word.

At Marshall High School, the basketball team is a lot looser. During Arthur's junior year, that looseness resulted in an embarrassing losing season. But the team starts strong during his senior year, winning four of their first six games. Now they face powerful Dunbar High School in their first game against a top Chicago team.

On the way to Dunbar, the Marshall players shout and clown around on the bus, like one big rolling party. Arthur plays poker with a group of friends in the back. "I'll bet a nickel," he says. "If I got a nickel." Coach Luther Bedford sits up front, staring straight ahead, lost in his own thoughts. He's more concerned about what they do on the basketball court than what they do on the bus.

Before the game, Coach Bedford tries to inspire the team to play their best against the highly favored Dunbar squad. "Only way you'll beat them is playing good basketball. You play half a game—for two or three minutes you play pretty good, then you go to sleep. You have to play a whole ballgame!"

The players nod in understanding, but when they take the court, Dunbar dominates the action. Part of the problem is Arthur, who has a tendency to slack off as the game goes on. "When we start off," Coach Bedford explains, "Arthur will be completely in the ballgame. But as the game progresses, then he digresses." In the middle of the first half, Arthur loses the ball on a sloppy, shoulder-high dribble, and Bedford pulls him from the floor. When Arthur sits down next to him on the bench, the coach chews him out and pantomimes how he's dribbling the ball way too high. Luther Bedford may not scream as much as Gene Pingatore, but he's no softie, either.

By halftime, Marshall trails Dunbar by fifteen points. But the Commandos show Coach Bedford that they've got more heart than he gives them credit for. They claw their way back into the game and tie the score late in the fourth quarter. On a crucial possession, Arthur drives down the left side and banks the ball into the basket to give the Commandos the lead. Marshall hangs on for a stunning upset.

In the locker room, Arthur Agee is the hero. He hugs one teammate, while another player recites a long list of nicknames they've given their star guard. As he reaches the end of the list, he holds his hand above his head. "I want it up high, 'Gee. I want it up high."

With a grin that stretches from ear to ear, Arthur reaches up and slaps his teammate a high, hard five. Marshall is on the move.

• A Struggle All Year •

Basketball was my ticket out of the ghetto.

—WILLIAM GATES

After his preseason problems, William regains his focus and averages sixteen points a game during the regular season. Once again, the Chargers dominate their competition, taking a record of twenty wins and only three losses into a late-season game against Carmel High School. At the end of the first quarter, Coach Pingatore calls out a play from the sideline: "Alabama! Alabama! Alabama!"

William tries to run the play, but he forces a pass and Carmel intercepts the ball in time for a desperation shot at the buzzer. The shot misses, but Pingatore is furious, and he gets even angrier when William complains about the play on the sideline. "Well, don't throw the ball!" he shouts as William walks off the court. "Jesus, will you cut it out and quit acting like a baby! Will you quit crying!"

St. Joseph's leads at the half, but Coach Pingatore isn't satisfied. He's not really worried about Carmel. He's worried about the upcoming play-offs, where the Chargers will face stiffer competition.

"This team just drives me crazy!" he screams, pacing back and forth at the front of the locker room during halftime. "It's been a struggle all year. You think you're better than you are. The two big guys are prima don-nas—they should be killing people. Gates is not moti-vated because, well, you know, this is a nothin' team. Well that's terrific." The coach's sarcastic tone makes it clear that he doesn't think it's terrific at all.

"For you people that are really agonizing, and you just hate all this stuff, all the hollering . . . if you don't make a turn, it will be over next week, so you won't have to worry about it. That's the point. I want to end this game in the next three-four minutes. Otherwise, it's going to be a ballgame. All right let's go get them. C'mon."

Coach Pingatore and the players touch their hands together and bow their heads in prayer. "Hail Mary, full of grace . . ."

As his players file out of the locker room, Pingatore tries to put his finger on what's lacking in his star. "William's just too nice of a kid. I don't know if he has the killer temperament. I don't know if he has the eye of the tiger. He's gonna need it when he goes to the next level. It's business, it's big bucks, and that's what the scholarship is for."

When they retake the floor for the second half, the Chargers play like they're on a mission. They totally dominate Carmel, and win by almost forty points. Up in the stands, Catherine sleeps through it all, with Alicia sleeping on her lap.

Catherine is frustrated with Coach Pingatore and the way he demands total commitment from his players. She wants more of William's time for Alicia and herself. During lunch with Alicia and William in the Gates's kitchen, she expresses her feelings. "His coach is stingy and selfish. He just wants William to run out there and play."

"He is not stingy and selfish," William replies. Although he also gets frustrated, he understands why Coach Pingatore demands commitment.

"Yes, he is!" Catherine insists. "The day she was going to be born, I told him he had to be there. I don't care what his coach said. I know the game was important, but this was more important. And his coach doesn't see it like that."

William was at Alicia's birth, and he considers it one of the greatest moments of his life. But the only reason he was able to be there was because Gordon Tech eliminated the Chargers from the state tournament. "I can't just miss a game, just because an incident occurs . . . unless it was a death or something like that."

"Something like that! This is a once in a lifetime thing . . . like the girl is born every day!"

"Especially around that time of the year, too—state tournament! That was simply out of the question." While her parents argue, Alicia squirms around on Catherine's lap and plays with a slice of bread.

"He tells me it will benefit us in the future," Catherine explains. "I'm like, what about now? He keeps saying, 'In the future.'"

"Basketball was my ticket out of the ghetto," William says seriously. "If I wouldn't be playing ball, I would not even be going to college."

"I'm going to school," Catherine points out. "I'm going to college, and I have a daughter. So what's my excuse?"

"The situations are much different," William insists.

Catherine refuses to budge. "No, it's not."

Later William, Catherine, and Alicia go into William's

room, which is plastered with posters of Michael Jordan. William has two turntables and a mixing board, just like a professional dee-jay, and he spins records as Alicia dances for her parents. "If things don't go well," he says, "I have to do something that excites me, not that bores me. What I like doin' is playing my music." With William still sitting at the turntables, Alicia saunters over to him, and the two of them dance together with big smiles. For a little while—lost in his music and his love for Alicia—William Gates can forget about basketball.

William calls basketball his "ticket out of the ghetto." His brother Curtis thought it would be his ticket, too, but after dropping out of college, he ended up right back where he started, living in Cabrini Green. Curtis has been unemployed for almost a year—a tough time for a young man with a wife and daughter. Finally, he manages to land a job at Encyclopedia Britannica, working as a shipping clerk in the warehouse.

"If it wasn't for William knowing Mrs. Wier," he admits, "I wouldn't even be here. 'Cause I walk through that door, first thing I see on the sign is 'No Openings'." The job pays a fairly low hourly wage, but Curtis knows it's the best he can hope for right now. "It ain't much better than a person without a college degree can get. So I feel like I'll be here for quite a while."

• The Life Cycle of the Butterfly •

Man, you remember I told you, whatever I start I finish.

—MRS. SHEILA AGEE

Arthur Agee also looks at basketball as his ticket out of the ghetto. But before he can get where he wants to go, he has to change his work habits—especially in school. Arthur is not dumb, but he likes to take the easy way out. "I don't believe when people say that school is hard," he says, "'cause the work wasn't hard for me. If I gotta do a report or something, and I don't like none of the topics, I just pick something that's simple."

For one report, Arthur decides to write about the life cycle of the butterfly. He thinks it's an easy topic, and he begins with a creative idea. "As the people bloom into another year, the butterfly also blooms," he reads to a visitor. "The butterflies are very beautiful flying objects. At the beginning the butterfly goes through changes . . ." Arthur stops reading the paper and explains impatiently, "Then I keep going, man. I just don't like to do that stuff. Then I just keep going on and on and I'll never stop."

Although Arthur thinks school is easy, his first semester report card indicates that he's failing two classes: Spanish and science. His mother is very concerned, and she goes to meet with his science teacher, Mr. Webb, a young black man with a neatly-trimmed beard.

"He rushes through his work," Mr. Webb explains. He shows Mrs. Agee the class records. "As you see, he's turning in his work. He just missed one assignment. But his test scores are pretty low. He got a ten on one test."

Mrs. Agee examines the scores very seriously. She's definitely not happy with Arthur's academic performance. "Would you do me a favor?" she asks. "When you see things slipping like this, would you give me a call and let me know?"

Mr. Webb nods and grabs his pen. "Let me make sure I have the right phone number."

"So I can stay up on top of this boy," Mrs. Agee continues, "because he'll tell you one thing . . . I say, 'Where are your books?' 'Oh, we didn't have to work on anything—it's in my locker.' See, he's going to have to start showing me something better."

After her meeting with the science teacher, Mrs. Agee discusses Arthur's failing grades with Coach Bedford. "He's probably on the borderline," Bedford tells her, "but with all that clowning, people just get mad. That's what I would do, too."

Mrs. Agee nods in agreement. "I'm gonna stay up on his behind," she says, drawing a laugh from the coach. "I told him we're paying $189 to St. Joseph for his transcript, and he got the transcript, and he ain't working. It ain't gonna happen like that."

Mrs. Agee has been going to school herself, taking a nurse's assistance class at a local community center. As she prepares to go to her graduation, she dresses in a starched white nurse's uniform and admires herself in a big wall-mirror. She is feeling good, and she hopes her own hard work will be an inspiration to Arthur. "Man," she says, "you remember I told you, whatever I start I finish. I'm not like some people I know." Arthur hands her a comb, and she does some last minute hair styling as she continues to make her point. "I don't need nobody to push me. All I got to have is the goal and the motivation and I'm ready."

As his mother talks and fixes her hair, Arthur pantomimes a series of jump shots, watching himself in the mirror over her shoulder. He knows what she's getting at—about goals and motivation—but he doesn't want to think about it.

"I wanted to be an RN nurse," she says, admiring her crisp uniform. "I've always had that dream." RN stands for "registered nurse." A nurse's assistance course does not make her an RN, but it's a step in the right direction. A step closer to her dream.

Before the graduation ceremony at the community center, Mrs. Agee meets with her instructor, Ms. Marshall, who happily reports the results of her final exam. "Sheila, you scored eighty-nine on your exam, and you're gonna get the highest grade point average."

"Really? Really?" Mrs. Agee hops up and down with excitement. "Lord, Lord, Lord, LORD!" Then she throws her arms around the instructor. "Oh, I love you, I love you, I love you! I'm so happy. Oh thank you, Ms. Marshall." The high grade guarantees that Mrs. Agee will receive an official certificate as a nurse's assistant, opening up new opportunities for a better job.

Ms. Marshall warmly returns Mrs. Agee's hug. "You did it yourself!"

"Oh, thank you, you're so good!" Suddenly, Mrs. Agee begins to cry tears of joy. Although she told Arthur she could do whatever she set out to do, the truth is that she had her inner doubts. "I didn't think I could do it." she admits.

"I knew you could do it," says Ms. Marshall.

"Yeah, you did. You gave me that belief in myself. You really inspired me to go on. Not just stop right here, but go further. And people told me I wasn't gonna be anything." Now the tears are streaming down Mrs. Agee's face, ruining her carefully applied makeup. But she doesn't care. For this day, this moment, she feels like the biggest success in the world.

As the graduation ceremony begins, a young girl with a lovely voice sings: "Tell me, why should the shadows fall? I sing because I'm happy. And I sing because I'm free." Most of the folding chairs for the audience are empty, but Arthur and Joe are there, with a bouquet of flowers for their mother in the seat beside them. When Sheila Agee's name is called, and she steps forward to receive her diploma and her official nurse's assistant pin, the two boys crank their arms in the air as if to say, Right on, Mom. Good job.

Mrs. Agee pumps her fist in the air, too. It's her day.

Arthur's day is coming. After their terrible 9-16 record during his junior year, the Marshall Commandos have made a dramatic turnaround, taking a 16-6 record into a late-season home game against west side rival, Westinghouse High. The gym is packed, with the band rocking out and the cheerleaders entertaining the crowd with slick routines. Arthur has emerged as the team's second leading scorer and assist man, and some local junior colleges have begun to take notice of Marshall's number eleven. A junior college would be Arthur's only choice unless he makes an incredible improvement in his grades and scores an eighteen on the ACT.

Independent scout Stan Wilson watches carefully as Arthur dishes a perfect no-look pass to a teammate in the right corner, setting him up for a jump shot. Later Arthur takes the ball himself, making an acrobatic move under the hoop for a one-handed lay-up.

"A lot of these kids won't talk to a junior college," Wilson admits, "until after they've seen the dream of Illinois and Nevada, Las Vegas, and Georgetown kind of fade. It's just too bad those kids don't realize, 'Hey, if I had an eighteen [on the ACT] the door is so much wider open.'"

Despite Arthur's stylish play, the Commandos trail by eleven points at the half. But once again, they fight their way back in the fourth quarter, narrowing the gap to a single point. During a time out, Coach Bedford demands that they get tough. "We got to play more aggressive on defense. We're not doing anything on defense!"

When the players retake the floor, they stick to their men like glue. "Defense!" Mr. Agee screams from the stands. A missed shot by Westinghouse leads to a rebound and a fast break by Arthur's fellow guard, Derrick Zinneman. As Zinneman drives down the court for a breakaway lay-up, Arthur's father jumps down from the stands to point the way. The gym explodes with cheers when Zinneman's lay-up drops through the hoop. Marshall leads by one with two minutes left in the game.

A few moments later, a Westinghouse player fouls Derrick Zinneman hard—so hard that the referee adds a technical foul to the regular foul. Then Westinghouse makes it worse by protesting the call, and the referee calls another technical. Suddenly Marshall has a golden opportunity. After Zinneman makes one of his two free throws for the original foul, the Commandos have two more free throws for the technicals. On a technical foul, a team may choose any player to shoot the free throws, and the player stands alone at the line, while the rest of the players wait in the backcourt. Arthur is Marshall's strongest free-throw shooter, so they send him to the line—all alone with a chance to put the game on ice.

Despite the pressure, he looks cool and calm. He takes a look at the basket, dribbles the ball four times, spins it backwards between his hands, and sets for the shot. Swish! The crowd roars as the ball drops through the net.

The noise continues as Arthur goes through his ritual for the second shot. "One more!" screams his father. But Arthur doesn't seem to hear him—or anyone else. He's in a world of his own. Four dribbles, spin the ball backwards, set and shoot. Swish!

Now Arthur shows the pressure. He turns upcourt and bends over, letting out a big, deep breath. Then he stands straight and tall to slap his teammates five. When the buzzer sounds for the end of the game, Mr. Agee and other Marshall fans rush out onto the floor and lift Arthur onto their shoulders. He reaches his arms high in the air and pumps with both fists. Victory is sweet.

In the locker room, the celebration continues. But Coach Bedford has a few sobering words. "Arthur Agee, you lead the books—you got seven—seven turnovers.

Even for the guards that's too much. This is a good win for you, but it doesn't mean anything. You've got to do better than that, man. You've got to do better than that."

Arthur doesn't let Bedford's criticism bother him—coaches are always talking like that after a good game. They always want you to play better. But back at home, his mother seems to criticize him, too.

"Yeah, Man, that was a good game. You could've played better though, you know." Mrs. Agee laughs, but it's hard to tell if she is serious. She and Arthur are sitting at the kitchen table, with Jazz crawling around on the table top. Tomika's there, too, and she sticks up for Arthur. "Ah, Mom, you know he did good. You just kidding . . ."

Now Mrs. Agee gives Arthur a warm smile and slaps him affectionately on the arm. "You know your mother's proud of you, don't you? He's been getting down like a real star."

• Where You Been, Man? •

chapter 23

I've got a bitter taste in my mouth about a lot of things that happened.

—EARL SMITH, unofficial scout

Almost four years after he discovered Arthur Agee on a city playground, Earl Smith comes to watch Arthur's first play-off game. "I figured this game or the next game may be his last high school ballgame," Smith says. But Earl's doubts turn out to be very misplaced. This game will not be Arthur's last, as the Commandos roll over their first round opponent. Afterwards, Earl offers Arthur a ride home, and they have a chance to catch up on the last four years as they walk out across the gym floor.

"Where you been, man?" Arthur asks.

"Where've I been?!" Smith laughs at the question— as if he was supposed to be following Arthur around for the last four years. "I've been working."

"Ah, yeah, right." Arthur sticks his hands into his gold, satin Marshall jacket. He looks so much taller, bigger, and more mature than he did four years ago.

"I've been following you in the papers," Smith says defensively.

"Ah, yeah. Are you impressed or something?"

"Yeah, I'm impressed," Smith replies, still laughing at Arthur's tough act. "I'm here, aren't I? If I wasn't impressed I wouldn't have followed you."

"Talk to Ping?" Arthur asks.

"For what?"

Arthur seems surprised. "You don't talk to him no more? Why not?"

Smith shrugs. "What do I have to talk to him about? You ain't there."

"Yeah, you're right. I had to break out."

"Yes," Smith replies, and glances quickly at Arthur to try and gauge what he's really thinking.

Outside it's dark and rainy as Smith guides his car through the slick city streets. "I was thinking about going tonight to see St. Joe and Nazareth play," he says to Arthur, sitting beside him in the wide front seat. "But I wasn't sure if you had time to do it or not."

Arthur has the time, and Smith makes the familiar drive out toward Westchester, thinking about Arthur and the other boys he has recruited for the suburban school. "I've got a bitter taste in my mouth about a lot of things that happened," he admits. "A lot of people accuse me of taking youngsters out of the inner city and taking them out to St. Joe's High School. And they ask what did I get out of the deal . . . a lot of racial slurs and so forth from my own people about me, about what I did." Smith pauses thoughtfully. This is a painful and difficult subject for him. "I still feel that I was doing the right thing for that particular time. Sometimes I have second thoughts when I see the net results of what happened with youngsters."

When they get to St. Joseph's, Arthur roams through the halls greeting old teachers and friends. He's in a great mood, happy to see everyone. Although he left in frustration, he doesn't feel frustrated today. He's a basketball star at Marshall, and they're in the play-offs just like St. Joe's.

One lady teacher doesn't recognize Arthur at all. "Arthur," he introduces himself politely, "Arthur Agee, sophomore."

Suddenly the teacher realizes who he is, and breaks into a warm smile. "My gosh, what are you doing? What are you doing now?"

"Going to school."

"Where?"

"Marshall."

She gives him a big hug, amazed by how tall he is. "Oh, I taught him. Can you believe it? That's good."

Arthur moves on and finds a bunch of old friends. They're happy to see him, too, and they all hug each other.

"You playing basketball or what?" asks one of the boys.

"Yeah."

"How'd you guys do?"

"We did all right," Arthur replies modestly. "We're still playing." In the Illinois high school play-offs, "still playing" is definitely all right.

On the way into the gym, Arthur passes the familiar glass trophy case devoted to Isiah Thomas. He's seen it a hundred times before, so he doesn't pay much attention. But he lingers for a while at another glass case. This one is full of newspaper clippings about the Chargers, and most of them feature pictures of William Gates.

Finally, Arthur sits down next to Earl Smith in the stands. St. Joseph's gym is rocking with excitement. The band is loud and the cheerleaders from a nearby girl's school are dancing down on the floor. Although most of the faces in the stand are white, the feeling in the gym is no different than the feeling at Marshall a few hours earlier. Play-off excitement is the same in the city and the suburbs.

Even though it's a big game, William starts off on the bench—a punishment from Coach Pingatore for arriving late to the locker room. St. Joe's is favored over Nazareth, but without William in the game, Nazareth starts strong and stays right with the Chargers. Leading the Nazareth attack is their own star, Sean Pearson, William's friend and roommate from the Nike Camp. Finally, Coach Pingatore sends William in and he quickly establishes control, driving around the taller Pearson for a lay-up.

With William in the game, the Chargers race to an early fourteen-point lead. But in the fourth quarter they begin to fall apart with missed shots and sloppy play. Once again, William steps up to take control. Driving into the crowded lane, he fakes out a defender with a behind-the-back dribble, makes the lay-up and draws a foul for a three-point play. Up in the stands, Arthur and Earl Smith smile in appreciation at the brilliant play.

But Sean Pearson responds with his own brilliant play. A few moments later, his three-point jump shot gives the Nazareth Roadrunners their first lead of the game. Nazareth hangs on, and the Chargers are still down by a point when they get the ball with just over a minute left in the game. Their entire season may come down to this possession. Faced with tough defense from the Roadrunners, the Chargers find William deep in the right corner. He blows by the outside defender and drives the baseline to face Pearson guarding the basket.

William pulls up for a soft five-footer over Pearson's outstretched arms. The ball bounces agonizingly around the inside of the rim, only to bounce out into Pearson's grasp. On the sidelines, Coach Pingatore grimaces—that was it, that was the shot.

In the final minute, Nazareth extends their lead to six. William misses a long, desperation shot at the buzzer, but it wouldn't have mattered anyway.

While the Nazareth fans cheer and celebrate the upset, William and the other Chargers walk off the floor with their heads hanging down. It's the earliest exit for the Chargers from the play-offs in six years. And for William Gates, it's a bitter end to a brilliant, yet frustrating high school career.

Afterwards, Curtis Gates expresses his opinion of the game. "Ain't but one thing—bad coaching. Bad coaching."

"We got him here five minutes late," says a friend.

"So what!" says Curtis. "This ain't no time to be teaching nobody no lesson."

Coach Pingatore offers a different view of the situation. "William was almost twenty minutes late. The team was dressed and already talking, and he came strolling in. Maybe he has to learn something from that, even in a big game."

After the players have showered, William emerges from the dressing room to find his family waiting for him—like a strange, painful repeat of his junior year loss to Gordon Tech. First he hugs his mother, trying to fight back his tears. Then he hugs his brother-in-law, Alvin—a tower of strength for him ever since his injury—and now he begins to cry. It hurts so much to go out a loser. But that's the way it goes in the Illinois play-off system, in any play-off system. Only one team wins; the others lose.

Tonight William finds someone else waiting for him with open arms. Someone who wasn't there last year. Someone who really understands. It's Arthur Agee.

"Hurt, don't it?" asks Arthur.

William nods, the tears still streaming down his face. "Man, more than ever. I didn't ever want to go out this way, man."

"Your last year, man," says Arthur, his voice full of understanding. "I'm trying to get it, man. I'm striving for the same thing. All right, man, I'm gonna call you." He circles William with his long arms and hugs him tight. "You played a good game, boy, all right. You gonna be all right. I love you, boy."

"I love you, too, man." With a firm squeeze, William breaks away from Arthur and leaves with his family.

In the locker room, Coach Pingatore sits alone, sipping his post-game can of Coke. He's seen more wins than losses in his years of coaching, but for all his great success, every single season has ended with a loss. That's the only way it can end, unless you go all the way to the state championship.

"The game was a mirror," Pingatore says, "a mirror of all the games all year. To quote Isiah, the toughest loss he ever took was my toughest, and that was the De LaSalle game in 1979, when we got beat at the buzzer on a thirty-footer, and we were favored to win state that year. Now I look back at it as one of those great moments in our high school scene—our toughest loss to take and we talk about it. So that's the way I look at these things now." Though philosophical about his loss, it is clear how much winning means to Coach Pingatore. It is on his face no matter what he says.

Suddenly, Arthur Agee enters the locker room to say hello. Coach Pingatore looks up from his thoughts with a warm smile. It seems like everyone at St. Joe's is happy to see Arthur today. "Arthur! Could've used you tonight."

"Yeah," says Arthur. It's only one word, but it says it all.

"Good luck. I'm gonna be watching. Hey, stay in touch."

Arthur leans down to give Coach Pingatore a hug, and the Coach reaches up to hug him back, standing up beside the boy. Arthur is now taller than the coach. "All right, I'm watching you score. How's your grades?"

"They're all right," Arthur replies with a shrug. Of course they're not all right, but he doesn't want to talk about grades tonight.

"Good. We missed you," Pingatore says, with real feeling.

"I missed you all, too." Arthur means it.

Coach Pingatore cocks his head to the side and smiles, as if he's seeing Arthur from a whole new angle. "I'm proud of what you've done. Mr. Bedford said a lot of good things about you. You be in touch. Okay? Good luck."

"All right. You too." As Pingatore watches, Arthur Agee walks out of St. Joseph's locker room for the last time. Before he leaves the school, he stops and takes a long look at the near-empty gym. It's a beautiful place, really. A place where dreams just might come true. William's dreams. Arthur's dreams. Hoop dreams. He could have played here alongside William, if only . . . if . . .

• City Champs •

Arthur Agee stood as still as a statue. Time after time was on his side.

—CHICAGO TRIBUNE

William's high school career is over, but Arthur and the Marshall Commandos are still going strong. In the second round of the play-offs, they easily defeat Manley High School. Marshall doesn't have a lot of size, but they're extremely quick—and the quickest of them all is Arthur. He seems to spend the whole game speeding downcourt on the fast break and driving in for uncontested lay-ups.

Up in the stands, Mr. Agee finds himself surrounded by college recruiters. A representative from Elmhurst College hands him a folder filled with information about the school, a private college located in the western suburbs. "This just explains a little bit about our program, where our program's headed."

Bo takes the folder and glances quickly through the materials. "I like what you're saying," he says politely, "and I want him close to home, you know. I'm kind of leaning your way, because I just thank God that he's getting into it—you know, somebody do want him."

But Elmhurst isn't the only school interested in Arthur. Another recruiter reaches over to shake Mr. Agee's hand. "I'm Tommy Travis—Northeastern Illinois assistant coach. Nice to meet you."

Mr. Agee smiles, a little surprised by all the attention. "Okay. I'm Arthur's father."

Now a third man reaches in to shake his hand. "I'm Arthur Hester. Us Arts got to stick together. I'm over at Kennedy-King."

"Kennedy-King?" asks Mr. Agee with a laugh. "Okay, may the best man win!"

After the game, the recruiters work on Mrs. Agee, trying to get on her good side. "I thought Mom was a cheerleader," says Tommy Travis, the coach from Northeastern Illinois.

Mrs. Agee knows he's laying it on pretty thick, but she enjoys the attention anyway. "Thanks!" she says with a big smile. "Thank you for the compliment."

After his conversation with the Agees, Tommy Travis talks with Luther Bedford outside the locker room. "His parents seem to think he may pass the ACT," he says, hopefully.

Bedford looks at the recruiter like he's crazy. "He may what?"

Travis laughs. "He may pass it."

"Oh yeah. Well I hope he does." Bedford shrugs and walks away. Obviously, he doesn't think there's much chance of Arthur getting an eighteen on the test.

Kennedy-King is a Chicago junior college, so they can recruit Arthur no matter what he scores on the test. The recruiter, Arthur Hester, figures he's got another advantage, too—his name. He stops Arthur in the hallway and introduces himself with a firm handshake. "Us Arts gotta stick together."

"Yeah," says Arthur with a grin. After all the struggles of the last four years, it feels good to be wanted.

Back at home, Arthur does some homework with Derrick Zinneman, his fellow guard on the Marshall squad. "Hey, would you get excited if a college coach came up and talked to you?" he asks.

"Not really," Derrick replies thoughtfully. "Really it just—you just going to another level of basketball, to me that's all. I'll be excited when I get there."

Arthur nods enthusiastically. "That's when you be excited the whole year. I'll be excited as soon as I step up in there. First day of practice."

Derrick looks down at his homework papers and mumbles something very quietly, as if he's almost afraid to say it out loud. "If I graduate, I think I'll be the only one in my family, besides my uncle, to finish college."

"Me, too," says Arthur.

The Marshall Commandos roll easily through the first three rounds of the play-offs. Their first real test comes in the fourth round, against heavily favored Taft High School, one of the toughest teams in the city. But the Commandos just keep on rolling, beating Taft by a score of 70-61. Arthur scores nineteen points, one of his best games of the season.

Afterwards, a couple of sports reporters interview Arthur. "Do you guys feel you can play with any team in the city?" one of the reporters asks.

Arthur answers confidently. "On any given day, we can play with anybody. We can beat anybody."

Now the Commandos are one of four public high schools still competing for the Chicago city champi-onship—and the city champion goes downstate for the state tournament. The championship games are held in the Chicago Amphitheater, a huge arena that has been used for everything from circuses and livestock shows to Boy Scout Jamborees. The wooden basketball court looks tiny on the floor of the enormous stadium, and the stands are a long way from the court. But the fans and bands and cheerleaders make some serious noise anyway. This is as good as it gets in Chicago Public League basketball.

In the semifinals, Marshall faces the ultimate test— King High School, rulers of the Public League. Last year, King won the Illinois state championship, and basketball experts called them the finest high school team in the nation. This year King has only lost one game while winning twenty-six.

The secret of King's success is its recruiting—finding the biggest and best grammar school players. But King's recruiting practices have put the public school at the center of a national controversy. Critics have accused King of seducing grammar school recruits with expensive basketball gear and convincing star players from other high schools to transfer to the school. Coach Bedford doesn't like the whole idea of recruiting.

"We don't understand what we're really doing to these young kids," he says seriously. "The kid's twelve years old, and you're baiting him to come to your school, you know, to play basketball. I'm not going to start recruiting in that manner. I'll probably get outta the game before then."

Bedford knows that his squad faces an uphill battle against the bigger, stronger King team. But he does his best to prepare them and sends them out to the floor. King's strategy is to go inside to their two seven-footers —high school boys big enough to be playing center in the NBA. At first, their size intimidates the Commandos. They dominate the inside and rebound their teammates' missed shots, dropping the ball through the basket as if it were a toy.

Only Arthur seems unfazed. On one play, he grabs a long rebound that bounces over the outstretched hands of the seven-footers. As soon as the ball touches his hand—before King knows what hit them—he explodes upcourt for an easy lay-up. You boys may be big, he seems to say, but you'll never catch me. Arthur's confident play and King's sloppy performance keep the game close during the first half.

As the second half begins, Mrs. Agee makes a hopeful prediction. "I think they're going to take it." Mr. Agee, dressed in a sweater and a tie, nods in agreement. But he looks tense.

Now King starts to play their game and grabs a four point lead. Coach Bedford calls a time-out before the lead gets any bigger. "You don't play with no confidence whatsoever!" he shouts. "None! None!" He isn't really angry, and his players know it. He's just asking them to play their very best. To believe that they can win.

When Marshall retakes the floor they play aggressive, in-your-face defense, going for the steal whenever King's slow big men handle the ball. On offense, the Commandos turn their superior speed into a flurry of fast-break points. Derrick Zinneman takes a full-court pass in the right corner and drives the baseline for an explosive lay-up, tumbling to the floor as the ball falls through the hoop and the referee calls a foul on the King defender. Derrick picks himself up and slaps Arthur a hard, high five. Up in the stands Mr. and Mrs.

Agee cheer with big smiles on their faces—maybe they really are gonna make it!

Late in the fourth quarter, Marshall surges to a six-point lead. During a time-out, Coach Bedford tries to calm them down. "We got a long time to play," he reminds them. Then he outlines a plan. He wants to force King out of their zone defense—where their big men block the middle—and make the taller, slower players match up man-to-man with Marshall's quick guards.

The team breaks their huddle and heads back out to the floor. Arthur brings the ball upcourt, but instead of passing or driving into the middle, he stops as soon as he crosses the half-court line and holds the ball, cradling it under his left arm. He stands like a statue—calmly, quietly—daring the King players to come out and get him. The defenders look over at their coach in confusion. He's confused, too, for a moment. Then he motions for someone to go out and cover Arthur. There's nothing else he can do. They're six points down, and the seconds are ticking away.

As soon as the big man is right in front of him, Arthur makes a quick move and dribbles easily around him. He drives toward the top of the key and makes a perfect bounce pass to his teammate cutting in from the left side. The teammate pulls up for a jump shot and nails it. Nothing but net.

It's all over for the former state champs. Now it's Marshall's turn to play for the city championship. Arthur runs across the hardwood floor and pumps his two fists high in a salute to victory.

In the winning locker room, Mr. Agee is just as

excited as the players. Arthur runs through the crowd and grabs his father's outstretched hand. But instead of just giving him a high five or a handshake, he jumps into his father's arms and hugs him tight. It's a special moment. For the first time, since Mr. Agee returned to the family, his oldest son is showing real affection for him.

Outside the locker room, Arthur hugs his mother. "I told you we could do it!" he exclaims. "I told you we could do it!"

Mrs. Agee is just as excited as her son. "I knew you were going all the way. I told you. Ooooh! This is your last year—you're going all the way!"

The next day, the Agees are thrilled to see Arthur's picture plastered all over the Chicago area newspapers. "They got the best shot of him," says Mrs. Agee, holding up the *Chicago Sun-Times*. "And it's great. That was a great shot wasn't it? But this one in the *Tribune* is what I really like." She sets the other paper down and picks up the *Chicago Tribune*. "Arthur Agee stood as still as a statue," she reads. "Time after time was on his side."

"You know," Mr. Agee laughs, "the championship that I missed when I was in high school, twenty-one years later I got a chance to get a championship through him."

The Agees are so proud of Arthur and what he's doing on the basketball court. After so much failure, so much frustration, they realize that success is what their son really needs. Because success brings more success. "You always try to build your children up," Mrs. Agee explains, her face glowing with happiness, "but you're really lying on the inside a little bit, because you know he's got a long haul. But this makes you even more confident, because if he's sure of himself you know you can bank on it."

For Mr. Agee, the win over King High School has another meaning that has nothing to do with basketball and nothing to do with success. "Yesterday, when he won the game," he recalls, "you know, he told me he loved me. And I haven't heard that in a . . ." Mr. Agee stops without finishing the sentence. He hasn't heard it in a long, long time.

In the city championship game, Marshall faces Westinghouse High School, the team they beat so dramatically earlier in the season. The game is televised in the Chicago area, but William comes down to the Amphitheater. He sits behind the Marshall band, with Catherine by his side. It's painful for him to watch with his season over, but he feels a loyalty to Arthur. He wants to show his support.

After the intense, down-to-the-wire drama of the semifinal game against King, Marshall could easily have a let-down. It happens all the time in sports—even to the pros. But the Commandos come out running and blow Westinghouse right out of the stadium. On a key possession, Arthur streaks out at the front end of the fast-break, and lays the ball right into the basket—as pretty as a picture.

"And now Marshall has busted this game wide open!" cries the announcer.

Up in the stands, Mrs. Agee turns to a friend. "Did you see it?" she asks. "Did you see it?"

The route continues and Marshall takes the city championship by a lopsided score of 58-38. When the final buzzer sounds, Arthur starts jumping up and down like a kangaroo. Then he stumbles toward center court, and sinks into a squat, hanging his head all the way to the wooden floor. Suddenly the emotion is too much, and the tears begin—tears of total joy. A Westinghouse player tries to help him to his feet, but Arthur resists. He's too embarrassed to let the others see his tears. Finally, he pulls himself together and rises to his feet.

When Arthur makes his way toward the stands, William jumps down and throws his arms around him. "What's up, man!" Arthur shouts. "Told you what I was gonna do!"

"I told you, boy!" says William happily.

A few minutes later, the Commandos pose for pictures, holding their city championship plaque and raising their right index fingers in the familiar sign that says, "We're number one!" All around them, the fans chant: "Marshall! Marshall! Marshall!"

The next day, a new photograph appears in one of the Chicago papers. It's a shot of Arthur Agee jumping into Derrick Zinneman's arms at the end of the championship game.

• The Giant Killers •

chapter 25

Marshall got here because of one reason—quickness.
The reason—Arthur Agee.

—TV SPORTSCASTER, during 1991 state tournament

Marshall holds a pep rally to send their team off with a bang. The gym is packed—just like it would be for a big game. "We're going, going downstate!" the cheerleaders chant. "We're going downstate! Now let's, let's celebrate! Now let's celebrate!"

Coach Luther Bedford steps to the microphone and asks the crowd, "What are we gonna be?"

"State champions!" they scream. The gym explodes with noise and stomping feet. Above the din, Bedford introduces his team, their team. "Your Marshall Commandos!" The players run out onto the floor to a thunderous ovation.

As they board the bus outside the school, the team is still caught up in the fever of the pep rally. "Take state! Take state!" chants one player. "Number one!" But after the bus pulls away from Marshall and takes them out of the city, they settle down to look out the window at the flat farmland covered with a thin dusting of snow. This is a new and exciting experience, something they've dreamed of for years. Some of them have never been out of the Chicago area before. Now they're heading to Champaign for the state tournament.

When they pull up outside the University of Illinois Assembly Hall, they know they've really hit the big time. A modern, circular building with a graceful, arching dome, Assembly Hall looks like a giant spaceship in a sci-fi flick. Inside, everything is first class, with thousands and thousands of seats, bright television lights, and a high-tech video scoreboard. When the teams take the floor, the atmosphere is electric.

Eight teams go downstate each year for the tournament—the Elite Eight of Illinois high school basketball. To take the state title, a team has to win three games, one on Friday night and two on Saturday. With the two games Marshall had to win in the city finals, that's five games in a week—a grueling schedule for any athlete. It's a real test that separates the best from the rest.

In their first game, the unranked Commandos meet Batavia High School, ranked third in the state. They've been an underdog all season, so that's nothing new. But the pressure of performing in front of a huge crowd with statewide media coverage gives Marshall the big-game jitters. They look out of sync and blow easy lay-ups.

"You got the easy shots—you got to make the easy shots!" Coach Bedford screams during a time out. "I can't shoot for you."

The Commandos' sloppy play continues throughout the first half. "Luther Bedford looks like he's about to commit suicide over there," says the TV announcer.

Even Mrs. Agee, who always believes in her son and his teammates, looks worried. "Y'all better get on your job, Commandos!"

"Batavia's got these guys on the run!" says the announcer. Things look bad—very bad—for the boys from Marshall, and Batavia jumps out to a nine-point lead at the half. Then suddenly, in the third quarter, the Commandos charge back, and the man who leads the charge is Arthur Agee.

"And a steal by Marshall! Agee—gonna take it all the way!" Arthur's steal and break-away lay-up energizes the team. Late in the fourth quarter, a Marshall forward pulls the same trick, and the tide turns for good. "Here we go. Picked him clean! Dale—Marshall leads! Marshall's first lead since the first quarter. Like a lightning bolt the Commandos have struck. Thirty-seven to thirty-six, Marshall leading Batavia . . ."

Back home in Chicago, William watches the game on television and breaks into a big smile. That's his boy— that's Arthur doing it the way it's supposed to be done.

When he was a freshman, Arthur thought William would be with him in the spotlight. "I always dreamed of me and William taking them downstate together. When I was at St. Joseph, maybe we could've went downstate and maybe we couldn't. But we did it when I'm at Marshall."

Now Arthur steals the ball again and explodes down court for another lay-up. The high-tech video screen flashes his name and number: ARTHUR AGEE #11. Up in the stands, Coach Gene Pingatore watches with mixed feelings as the boy who got away dazzles the downstate crowd. He's happy for Arthur, but he can't help but wonder . . . what if?

Arthur's clutch performance helps lead the Commandos to an upset, a come-from-behind victory over Batavia. In his post-game press conference, Coach Luther Bedford labels his unranked team, "The Giant Killers."

Before the next game, the Agee family has a chance to enjoy the atmosphere of Champaign, a college town in the middle of the cornfields. Arthur is busy with the team, but Mr. and Mrs. Agee have Joseph to keep them company. Over breakfast at McDonald's, they chat with three fans from another school. They're much older than the Agees—maybe they're grandparents—and they're middle-class white people who seem to come from a small town. But they share something very important with the Agee family: a powerful pride in the achievements of their high school basketball team.

"You all are playing the number one, and we're playing the number two team," Mr. Agee tells them.

"This is the first time in the history of the school that we've gone this far," one of the ladies announces.

"Really?" asks Mrs. Agee.

"In the history of the school!"

"It's like the Commandos," says Mrs. Agee. "We being the underdog. I'm glad we are, because it just shows you how you can come up. And then you beat your opponent!" Mrs. Agee reaches over to slap the lady's hand, and the woman gives her a hard, low five. The whole group laughs at the joy of being downstate, and having that once-in-a-lifetime chance at the championship, and at how much joy basketball can bring people of such different backgrounds.

After breakfast, the Agees take a stroll through the beautiful campus—stately brick Colonial-style buildings surrounded by open spaces and trees. It's so quiet and pleasant and clean. So different from the west side of Chicago. "This'd be a good place for Man to come," says Mr. Agee.

"Yeah," Mrs. Agee agrees. "This is something that a child would miss out on. Like a whole different world."

"It's beyond different," adds Joseph. In his young life, he's never seen anything like it.

In the semifinals, Marshall is slated to play Peoria Manual, ranked number two in the state. Peoria is led by high school All-American guard, Howard Nathan, another boy who shared pizza with William back at Nike All-American Camp. But Marshall has a pretty talented guard of their own.

Before the game, the TV announcers profile the top players—past and present. "In this semifinal game, we'll see some great individuals, just as we saw many years ago. Remember Isiah Thomas—one of the great guards. Here you'll see the same moves he plays with in the NBA today. Well, we've got someone like that— Howard Nathan, number thirty-four for Peoria Manual."

The television picture switches from video clips of Isiah Thomas and Howard Nathan to two sportscasters standing out on the hardwood floor. "Marshall got here because of one reason," one of them says. "Quickness. The reason—Arthur Agee." Now they show clips of Arthur on the fast break. "Look at this man—he just explodes, Dan! He can get downcourt as quick as anyone I've ever seen."

When the game begins, Arthur goes head-to-head with Howard Nathan. It's a tough matchup, but Arthur gives it all he's got.

"Make him work for it, Man!" Mr. Agee screams, as Arthur uses his quickness to stay in Nathan's face. "Make him work for what he gets!"

On the other end of the court, Arthur follows a teammate's missed lay-up off the fast break. He grabs the rebound and goes right up with it, banking the ball in for two.

"All right, Man, let's go! Yeah! That's him, that's him!" For Arthur's dad, watching his son is almost as good as playing the game himself.

Later, Arthur handles the ball at the top of the key. He drives across the free throw line, makes a quick move and shoots. "Arthur Agee, spinning inside," says the announcer. "Tough shot—good!"

Arthur plays a great first half, but the Peoria Manual Rams play even better. No matter what Arthur does, Howard Nathan finds a way to score.

At halftime, the Commandos find themselves in a familiar position—down by nine, the same uphill battle they faced against Batavia the night before. They came back then. Can they come back again?

In the second half, Arthur tries to pick up where he left off. He drives the baseline and tries to force a shot from underneath the basket. "Little penetration move by Agee—slapped out of there by Manual," the announcer says. "They've got two-on-one. Oh! Nice fake and a score!" The Rams have the tired Commandos on the run, and Luther Bedford calls a time-out.

"You're not even in the offense at all," Bedford tells Arthur. "You're just out there playing individual basketball. Completely." Even in the tense atmosphere of the state championships, Coach Bedford doesn't shout or scream. He isn't really angry at Arthur—he knows the boy is playing his heart out. But he also knows that Peoria Manual is just too strong. Arthur can't do it alone. The only hope is good, solid team basketball.

After the time-out, Arthur tries to slow it down, handling the ball on the outside and calling set plays. But Peoria Manual refuses to fold. They just keep coming on strong.

"Marshall showed us last night they have the ability to come back," says the announcer. "Let's see what they can do here." But Howard Nathan takes it to them. He drives down the middle and makes a perfect no-look pass from the free-throw line, hitting a teammate streaking in on the right wing for a basket.

"Knocked it down!" the announcer shouts. "Biggest lead of the game now and the Ram fans can smell it." As the Peoria Manual fans dance in their seats, the video scoreboard flashes: MANUAL "RAMS." Amid the celebration, Mr. and Mrs. Agee and the rest of the Marshall fans sit somberly—no shouts now. Nothing but disappointment.

"It's been a great run for Luther Bedford's team, but the string of upsets stops here."

Down on the floor the game continues. Arthur reaches in to try to strip the ball away and gets called for the foul. It's his fifth and final foul of the game, the last game of his high school career. As he walks off the court, his name flashes on the television screen all over the state of Illinois: Arthur Agee 12 points.

"He fouls out," says the announcer, but his voice is full of admiration. "He just never quit; he just kept going for the basketball. I wouldn't be surprised if he made the All-Tournament team tonight."

As his parents watch sadly, Arthur walks slowly to the bench and slumps to his seat, holding a towel over his face. Either he's crying or it's just too painful to watch. He peeks over the towel to see his name flashing in giant letters on the video scoreboard: #11 ARTHUR AGEE.

By the end of the game, Mrs. Agee gets her spirits back. "Number One!" she shouts, holding her finger in the air. "We're still Number One."

When the buzzer sounds, Arthur walks across the wooden floor and shakes hands with the players from Peoria Manual. He gives Howard Nathan a quick hug, and keeps on walking to the locker room.

Although they were beaten in the semifinals, the Marshall Commandos finish third in the state of Illinois, the highest finish for a Marshall team since 1960. After the players have showered, Coach Bedford tries to sum up what this season means to the underdogs from the inner city. The players dress as they listen, putting on nice shirts and pants and jewelry to go and meet the media at the postgame press conference.

"This was a great season you had," says Bedford. "There's nothing sweeter than going downstate as a young person. I mean the record's gonna stay there. Nineteen ninety-one, there was a team from Marshall that played, you know, and you're part of that. That's part of history."

The team cheers at their coach's word—history. Standing in front of his locker in a fancy, patterned shirt, Arthur flashes a big grin as he fastens on a gold earring.

"You know, best wishes to all you seniors in whatever you try to do," Bedford continues. "Mr. Williams and I will be around school—as we always are—to help you . . . if you want to be helped."

At the postgame press conference, Coach Bedford stands at a podium on a raised platform and answers questions from twenty or so reporters sitting before him. When the coach is finished, Arthur Agee steps to the microphone. In the glare of the bright lights, he speaks with surprising confidence—as if he's been doing it all his life. "Like Coach said, you've just got to sacrifice, you know, sacrifice everything you have. If you love the game of basketball, you just go out there and give all your heart."

As Arthur speaks, Coach Bedford stands beside him on the platform. He isn't a man who smiles often, but now a slight smile appears on his face. Bedford always thought that Arthur goofed around too much to play up to his full potential. But Arthur Agee showed him something over the last few weeks. "You know, he's got a little way to go," the coach says later, "but he's gonna get there. Hopefully, he got his head screwed on pretty good, and now he's gonna be on his own to do whatever. Hopefully, he'll do it right."

After the press conference, a few reporters corner Arthur to ask more questions. Arthur is obviously enjoying the media attention, and the more he talks, the more confident he sounds. "When we got down here, people never expected anything: 'Marshall—how'd they get down here? Who they got on their team?' And I just had to come out and prove myself who I was."

While the reporters write down everything Arthur says in their little notebooks, Mrs. Agee watches from a few feet away. A smile lights up her face, too, a smile of pride and amazement and wonder. Right before her eyes, her boy is becoming a man.

"I think I can play Division I basketball," Arthur tells the reporters. "That's all I need is just a scholarship."

• Make It Rain •

Now when you make this decision, you got to live and die with it.

—ARTHUR AGEE, SR., to Arthur Agee, Jr.

Arthur may be able to play Division I basketball on the court, but he can't get a scholarship to a Division I school because he doesn't have the required grades or test score. In fact, he can't get an athletic scholarship to any four-year school. He has to go to a junior college.

Arthur's first recruiting visit is to Mineral Area Junior College, a modern, well-equipped facility in the rolling green countryside of southern Missouri. About fifty miles south of St. Louis, the school is located in the small town of Flat River, population 4,443—the kind of town where they advertise the flower and garden show with a big banner stretched across Main Street. It's about as different from the west side of Chicago as a place can be.

Mineral Area basketball coach Tim Gray gives Arthur a tour of the school, including the new computer labs. Despite its sleepy southern location, everything at Mineral Area looks clean and up-to-date, very different from the old facilities at Marshall High School. The gym is different, too—much bigger and brighter. But it's tiny compared to the enormous arena at the University of Illinois where Arthur played during the state championships. Or the arena where William will be playing at Marquette. "This is where it all happens," Gray says in his slight southern drawl. "It's a beautiful place. And it gets to rockin'."

Along with his tour of the school, Gray sets Arthur up for a number of interviews with the academic staff—people who don't talk to him about basketball at all. An English professor gives Arthur his own perspective on what the school is all about. "The strength I see here is the tremendous teaching that goes on here. Have you decided what you want to get into?"

Arthur is a little shy and surprised at the question. He hasn't done a lot of thinking about any goals other than basketball. "Uh, communications," he says vaguely.

A guidance counselor asks him to be more specific. "Are you more interested in the overall communications?"

"You know . . . that," Arthur replies, "and, uh, I like that and accounting, like business."

Next, Arthur meets the president of the college, a middle-aged man in a suit and tie. While Arthur sits on a couch in his office, wearing a White Sox cap and a Charlotte Hornets jacket, the president stands behind his desk and gives the prospective student the real message of the whole trip. "We enjoy winning things," he says pleasantly, "but the primary purpose is your education. What are some of your career goals, may I ask?"

By now, Arthur has had some practice, and he answers more clearly and confidently. "I want to fall back to like having my own business, like real estate."

Finally, Arthur meets with Coach Gray in his office. Gray is a young man—maybe in his early thirties— with a thick black moustache and brush-cut hair. His approach to recruiting is very different from the way that Kevin O'Neill recruited William for Marquette. No room service at the Hyatt. No balloons on the ceiling or phony tapes and newspapers. Mineral Area Junior College is not big-time basketball. But it's good basketball and a good opportunity.

"You need to be very careful with this decision," he tells Arthur, "'cause you're gonna have to live with it for two years."

Sitting casually, with his hands laced behind his head, Arthur nods seriously.

"You know, if you come in and act right, you're going out of here with two years of your college finished, a scholarship to a Division I university—exactly where you'd want to be, on track to graduate in four years."

From the coach's office, Arthur calls his mother back in Chicago. "It's nice," he tells her. "You should come down here and see it. It's like Alabama—country." At one time, Arthur dreamed of playing at the University of Alabama. But right now, Mineral Area looks like the next best thing.

Afterwards, one of the basketball players drives Arthur out to see where he would be living. The junior college doesn't have dorms, but it does have the basketball house—a simple, one-story brick house that sits all alone, surrounded by endless grassy fields. All the ball players on scholarship live in this house. And for this semester at least, that includes six of the seven black students in the entire school.

Inside, the house seems even smaller than it appears on the outside, with a dark, narrow hallway down the middle and a series of bedrooms on either side. One of the players, Myron Gordon, tells Arthur that it takes a little time to feel at home. "You come in and look at this little house—then after a while you get used to it. Try to make it a little home, you know. A home away from home anyway." Myron is a handsome, likable guy a year or two older than Arthur. "We hang around each other most of the time," he says, "We know who to trust and who not to trust."

Arthur heads back to Chicago with a good feeling about Mineral Area. But even though he understands the school's emphasis on education, the decision comes down to the one thing he really loves. "I just want to go somewhere I'm going to play," he says. "I can get the grades. I just love basketball."

A few weeks later, Coach Tim Gray visits the Agees up in Chicago. He's brought the official papers for Arthur to sign, accepting the scholarship and committing to attend the junior college. But first Mrs. Agee has some questions for him.

"How many of your players that leave there end up going to a four-year college?"

"Thirty-one sophomores in a row," Gray answers proudly.

"Really?" Mrs. Agee is obviously impressed.

"Every last one of them he coached," Arthur adds. Even though he's never been a big fan of school, Arthur's pretty impressed himself.

Very quietly, Mr. Agee enters the room. Coach Gray stands up to introduce himself, and they shake hands. "Arthur, Senior," says Mr. Agee, using his more formal name. His voice is low, and he's obviously uncomfortable at the situation. After trying to put their marriage back together, Mr. and Mrs. Agee have temporarily separated again. He's only there today because Mrs. Agee asked him to come and share this important decision in their son's life. Arthur didn't want him to come.

Mr. Agee perches on the back of the living room couch, hovering above Arthur's right shoulder. Coach Gray sits back down and pulls the papers out of his case. "I'll show you exactly what the scholarship entails."

"Is this a full scholarship for the two years?" Mrs. Agee asks. "The reason I'm skeptical is because of the promises that were made in the past."

"From the time he comes down there until he leaves," Gray assures her, "he will not have a financial need."

As Arthur and Mrs. Agee consider the offer, Mr. Agee offers some advice. "Now when you make this decision, you got to live and die with it. 'Cause it's your decision to make. Now I'm here to support you if you done searched this whole thing."

"And it's what you really want," Mrs. Agee adds. "Not because Mama said this or . . ."

". . . because you're saving Mama money." Mr. Agee finishes his wife's sentence. "'Cause if we have to, we will still pay—have to try to pay . . ."

When Mr. Agee starts talking about paying, Arthur rolls his eyes like his father's completely crazy. Mrs. Agee looks disgusted, too. They all know that they can't afford to pay for Arthur's college education—and Mr. Agee is the one who wasted a lot of money on drugs. But right now, at least, the older man is just trying to tell his son that no one is forcing him to make this decision. It's a free choice. It's up to Arthur.

"You have to do what's best for Man," says Mrs. Agee.

"Well, what do you think?" asks Coach Gray. Arthur mumbles something, but no one can hear it. He seems overwhelmed by this decision—especially since his parents are making it out to be so serious. "Ready to sign it?" Gray asks again.

"Yeah," Arthur says quietly.

"Let's do it up." Coach Gray sets the paper before him and Arthur carefully signs his name. Arthur looks off for a moment and wonders what his future at Mineral Area will bring.

Later, Arthur plays his dad in a game of one-on-one at the local playground, with family and friends gathered around to watch. Everyone is in good spirits now, and Mrs. Agee even roots her husband on. "Come on, Bo, whip it to him!"

Mr. Agee holds the ball at half court and does a little trash-talking. "When I was twenty-three, how old was he? And I whipped him then." He drives quickly toward the middle and makes a little bank shot over Arthur's outstretched arms. Then he takes the ball at half court again and stops about twenty feet from the basket. "You want to see it rain?" he asks with a laugh. "Let it rain!" He releases a beautiful arching jump shot that gets nothing but net. Swish! "You want to see it rain? Let it rain!" Another jump shot. Swish! "You want to see it rain?" This time he drives the middle and throws up a quick running shot, but it bounces off the rim, drawing laughs from the crowd.

Arthur grabs the rebound and takes the ball back to half court. Bo goes out to guard him, trying to distract him with more trash-talk. "Peoria Manual—remember what they did to you now. Do you know Howard Nathan?"

Arthur calmly dribbles the ball back and forth between his legs and goes up for a jump shot. "And I stuck him up just like that," he says. Swish! Two for Arthur, Junior.

Now Arthur drives in for an easy lay-up. "Like father like son," shouts someone from the crowd.

"You better stick to church music," teases Arthur's girlfriend, Edonnya. "Leave that basketball alone."

As the game goes on, Arthur takes the lead and the action gets more intense. They're playing to thirty-four, and when Arthur leads thirty-two to twenty-eight, Mr. Agee is up against the wall. Arthur drives in for a lay-up, and his father creams him with a hard foul.

"Hack! Hack!" screams the crowd. "Bo, you can't do that."

Arthur takes the ball at half court and drives again. Mr. Agee fouls him again, pushing him right off the court. But this time, Arthur makes the basket to win the game. Or so it seems.

Mr. Agee doesn't see it that way. "That didn't count because he called foul," he claims.

"That's thirty-four!" shouts Arthur. All of a sudden, the rivalry between father and son explodes in a shouting match over the score. It's half in fun—and half in anger. "Ain't no con game," Arthur says. "I'm older now. Ain't no con game going on no more."

"Losers quit," snarls Mr. Agee. "I'm ready to play. You're a coward if you don't play."

"He's mad now," says Arthur with a devilish grin.

"Give me the rock!" Arthur takes the ball at half court and pulls up for a long jump shot.

"Make it rain!" shouts Bo.

"Make it rain!" Arthur echoes. "Watch this." He releases the ball in a graceful arch and watches as it drops through the hoop. Swish! Nothing but net. This time it's Arthur who can talk the trash. "Game! Game! Right there! Go get down. Go sit down."

While Mr. Agee nurses his bruised ego, Edonnya walks by with an open umbrella—on a perfectly clear afternoon. "Bo! It's raining, Bo," she teases. "It's raining!"

• The Score I Needed •

Basketball was just like he was possessed with it. It was his life, and he wanted it to be everybody else's life, too.
—WILLIAM GATES, describing Coach Gene Pingatore

William made his college choice long before Arthur made his. But William's choice comes with a catch—he has to score an eighteen on the ACT. After taking the test for the fourth time, he's still shy of the magic number. Dennis Doyle, who is a guidance counselor as well as the assistant basketball coach, calls William into his office to discuss the situation.

"In order to play at Marquette, you're gonna have to get the eighteen," Doyle tells him. "And they're very, very concerned. One assistant called twice this week, and Bo Ellis called today."

William sits beside Doyle's desk, staring down at the floor.

"Smile, William. It's not the end of the world. Right?"

"I hope not." William manages a weak smile.

"Well, you've got to work at this as hard as you worked on your jump shot. And it was missing a lot this year." Doyle laughs at his little joke, but William doesn't think it's very funny. "Now you are down to the final inning and the last strike."

William feels depressed and overwhelmed; he keeps trying but he just can't get the score he needs. A high school student is only allowed to take the ACT five times. If he doesn't score an eighteen on the next test, he loses his scholarship to Marquette.

In the meantime, life goes on. On a rainy evening, the St. Joseph's basketball awards dinner is held in the banquet room of a local Italian restaurant. Coach Pingatore starts the proceedings off, his voice husky from a combination of pipe smoking and yelling on the sidelines. "Good evening, ladies and gentlemen, and welcome to St. Joseph's Annual Basketball Awards Dinner. We had a difficult year, most of you are aware of that . . ."

As the coach continues to speak, William sits at his table—with Catherine sitting beside him—and thinks about just how difficult the year was. But the difficulty for William Gates was not the same difficulty that Coach Pingatore is talking about. "When I first went to St. Joseph's," he recalls, "I really did sleep, eat, and drink basketball—that's all I did. But it became more of a job than a sport to play. Coach Pingatore just had these dreams in his head. He just wanted me to go the same route he took Isiah."

At the podium, Coach Pingatore is introducing the most valuable player on the St. Joseph Chargers. ". . . the most steals. He played as a freshman—not even Isiah was a four-year starter. One of the hardest workers on the team. All-conference in the SCC. All-State in the Sun-Times. McDonald's All-American nomination. MVP 1990–1991 season: William Gates."

As the audience applauds, William rises to his feet and walks across the crowded room to accept his award. He looks sharp in a gray double-breasted sport coat, and the smile on his face seems genuine. He is proud of his accomplishments. But there's a tension underneath the surface—a deep frustration with Coach Pingatore and the whole St. Joseph's basketball program.

"When I had some real problems," William says later, "I couldn't go to none of them about it. I was having some problems with Catherine's family, and my family, and the only thing Coach Pingatore could say is, 'Write 'em off.' That was all he told me. Now what kind of advice is that?"

The tension is still there when William says goodbye to Coach Pingatore at the end of the school year.

"Well, how's it feel—to be finishing?" Pingatore asks.

William scratches his head as if he doesn't know what to say. "Now that it's all over, and I can just . . . I mean, I enjoyed my four years here, and . . ." William's voice trails off as he searches for the right words.

The coach smiles. "Now don't say anything you don't mean, William."

"I'm serious, Coach. I enjoyed my four years. I mean, we had our run-ins."

"Who had run-ins?"

"Me and you."

"We did?" Coach Pingatore asks innocently, as if he has no idea what William is talking about.

"Yeah. Like that time you made me run seventy-five stairs."

Pingatore smiles knowingly. "You never forgot that. See, you should have been happy and enthusiastic about doing your punishment."

William scratches his head again and grimaces. He doesn't say anything, but it's clear he doesn't agree with the coach's ideas about punishment.

"But someday you're gonna learn that everything that was done was for your benefit," Pingatore continues. "So that you can come back four years from now and say, 'Coach, you were right. Everything that happened at St. Joe's helped me a lot. And as a result, I got a degree.' That's what I'm hoping for."

"I'm going into communications so when you start asking for donations, I'll know the right way to turn you down." Both Coach Pingatore and William laugh nervously. William has always had a good sense of humor, and he says it as if it were a joke. But there's something a little nasty in his voice.

"I'm sure you'll never turn us down." Coach Pingatore and William rise from their chairs and begin to walk toward the door. When William says good-bye, the coach shakes his head. "It's never good-bye," he tells him warmly. "I'll always stay in touch. I'm proud of what you did. I expect you to do a lot better. I don't want this to be the highlight of your career. You have a lot of bigger and better things to do. I'll see you later. Good luck!"

Coach Pingatore watches William walk out the door of his office. Then he shrugs his shoulders and heads back to his desk. "Well, another one walks out the door, and another one comes in the door. That's what it's all about."

While William strolls down the long hallway, past the Isiah Thomas trophy case, Coach Pingatore reflects on the career of the boy he thought might someday stand beside Thomas in the history of St. Joseph's High School. "I never really felt that he bought into the system. He was never convinced what he was doing was the right thing to do. But overall he had a good career. Not a great career. Could've been different if the injury didn't occur. But it did occur, and that was the big difference."

A few days later, with his family watching proudly, William marches down the aisle of the St. Joseph chapel to the stately sounds of "Pomp and Circumstance," the song traditionally played at graduation ceremonies. The St. Joseph graduates wear red gowns, the same color as the Chargers' basketball uniforms. William receives his diploma with a handshake from the school president, who is wearing a fancy academic gown. Coach Pingatore stands beside the president, also wearing an academic gown and looking very different than he looks on the sidelines.

After the ceremony, William's family gathers around him outside the chapel. William hands his new diploma to his mother, a gift from a loving son to the woman who kept him going through good times and bad times. Mrs. Gates wraps him in her arms and holds him close. This is one of the proudest moment of her life.

"I think my Mom was proud of me all through high school," William says later. "She said, 'Everybody's throwing their dreams into you. But you got to throw your own dreams into yourself.'"

Little Alicia and Catherine hug William, too. They're both proud of him. But the longest hug of all comes from Curtis. He circles his little brother in a big bear hug and just squeezes him and squeezes him like he's never going to let him go. As Curtis whispers in his ear, William begins to cry with joy. He understands why this is such a special moment for Curtis. "Curtis always wanted to go to Marquette, and his grades weren't good enough to go. Now it's like he got the grades."

But even though William got the grades, he still can't accept the scholarship until he scores an eighteen on the ACT. William takes the test for the fifth time a few weeks after his graduation. Then, on the fifth of July, a letter arrives at the Gates' home in Cabrini Green. It's an oversized envelope, and the return address says: ACT. William sits on his bed and opens the envelope slowly, carefully, nervously. His future depends on what's inside.

He pulls out the computer printout and scans it quickly. Across the top of the page it reads: 1990–91 ACT Assessment Student Report. There are lots of numbers for different parts of the test, but only one number really matters now. William's eyes focus on the composite score, and he shakes his head like he can't believe it. He looks at the number again. It's still there. For real. Composite: 18.

Now William breaks into a big smile and flaps the paper in the air. "It came through for me! I got the score I needed. Hey, I'm eligible. You know, it's one of the greatest feelings in the world!"

Later, William carries a small, old suitcase out to the dumpster behind his building. He opens the suitcase and dumps out all the recruiting mail he has received from other colleges. Then he throws the suitcase in for good measure. The agony of waiting and wondering is over. He's heading for Marquette.

• Bye, Mom •

*To my son—I hope you pursue all your dreams and
your desires . . . and I love you very much.*

—MRS. SHEILA AGEE

Before Arthur can graduate from high school he has to
pass one more session of summer school. But for the
first time in three years, his friend Shannon isn't there
to keep him company.

"He thought he could sell drugs and don't get caught,"
Arthur explains bitterly. "But he found out the hard
way. And I told him, while he was doing all that, I
wasn't hanging with Shannon. I was like, 'Shannon,
man, you should stop doing that stuff.' We always said
we weren't going to do no stuff like that. We were just
going to graduate and go on to college. But you know,
he had to be the one."

Arthur passes summer school and looks forward to
his graduation. But a week before the ceremony, he gets
another bitter taste of inner-city life. While driving his
girlfriend Edonnya's car, he pulls into a gas station to
make a phone call. When he gets back into the car, two
men are waiting for him with a gun. The thieves not
only take the car, they steal Arthur's clothes, forcing
him to walk home in his underwear.

"At first I thought he was going to shoot me 'cause I
didn't have no money," Arthur explains. His voice is

deadly serious, without a trace of his usual joking. "'Cause he kept asking me, you know, you got some money? Where your wallet at? And what you driving a car like this for? And I ain't got no wallet. And then you know he grabbed me and stuff, and I was about to panic, and I just calmed down. I was just hoping that he wasn't gonna shoot me."

Mr. Agee sits beside Arthur, listening. His face is deadly serious, too. He knows the dangers of the streets from personal experience, and he doesn't think his children really understand that it's life or death out there—that people are desperate for money and they'll pull a gun on anyone who looks like they've got something worth stealing. Arthur isn't the only family member who's recently faced the hard reality of the streets; his sister, Tomika, was also stopped at gunpoint.

"I sat down and had a long talk with him and his sister. Someone pulled a pistol on her right down the street from the house. I said, do you all understand what is going on out here in these streets today? In one week, I could have lost my two oldest children." Mr. Agee pauses for a moment, thinking about how he was once part of the problem that he's now trying to protect his children from—back when he was hooked on drugs. "When I was out there, you know—out there strung out—I looked for somebody that looked like they had something."

For Arthur, the robbery is a sign that he's doing the right thing by getting out of the inner city and going to school in a completely different environment. "After this, I'm ready to leave," he says, hugging a soft, colorful, plush basketball in his arms. "'Cause there ain't nothin'—everybody up here either going to jail or in drugs . . . or dead."

Arthur graduates in a big ceremony with all the other summer school graduates in the city of Chicago. He wears a blue graduation gown and a traditional mortar-board hat with a tassel dangling to the side. The graduates file into the auditorium to a modern song sung by one of their peers, a black student with a strong, beautiful voice. "In this very room," he sings, "there's quite enough hope and quite enough power to chase away any gloom. For we are the future. We are the future. And we're here in this very room . . ."

The audience is supposed to hold their applause until the end of the ceremony. But when Arthur's name is called and he walks across the stage to receive his diploma, the applause and cheers threaten to drown out the names of the other graduates. He is a popular young man, with lots of family and friends there to root for him, just as they rooted for him on the basketball court. Mr. Agee smiles proudly, but the proudest of all is Arthur's mother. She can barely control her excitement. "I never thought he would get to the place where he's at now. Arthur's self-esteem was really drained from St. Joseph's. I said, 'Well, you are somebody. No matter where you go, it's what you have in your heart.'"

Before William and Arthur leave for college, their families throw going away parties for them. William's party is a barbecue in Peggy and Alvin's back yard. There's lots of food and a big cake that says: Congratulations William—Marquette. There is a dee-jay, too, who gets the partygoers into the right mood.

"Everybody out there, there's gonna be a party tonight! There's gonna be a party tonight! You know it!"

Catherine shows William some new dance steps, and he catches on fast, laughing and having a great time. Later, William does a line dance with Alvin and a bunch of other young men. They've all got the steps down, dancing in perfect synchronization until William throws in an extra move of his own—a quick fadeaway jump shot.

Arthur's party is held in the Agees' flat, with lots of wild dancing in the living room. Derrick Zinneman, Arthur's friend from the basketball team, is there. So is Shannon, who has recently gotten out of jail. As Mr. Agee watches the younger people dancing to the beat, he shakes his head as if he suddenly feels very old. "It's scary, man, I'm telling you. I'm telling you the truth. It's a scary generation."

In the kitchen, Arthur pops the cork on a bottle of champagne, and the cork flies a little too close to his mother's head.

"Told you, you might hit me in my head, fool!" Mrs. Agee teases.

"Didn't hit you in your head!" says Arthur.

When the champagne is poured, Mrs. Agee raises her glass in a toast. "To my son—I hope you pursue all your dreams and your desires that you have within you, and I love you very much."

Later, Arthur does a funky, feelin'-good dance between two lines of friends, and Mrs. Agee follows him with her own funky strut. Arthur laughs at his mother's dance and wraps his arms around her in a big, warm, silly hug.

The next day, Coach Tim Gray arrives to drive Arthur down to Mineral Area. The coach stands respectfully at a distance as the Agee family gathers in a circle, holding hands in a final prayer. "God, we thank you for this day, Lord," says Mr. Agee. "And we ask you to go with Junior, Lord. Go with him as he tries to better his education, Lord. And we thank you for coming this far, Lord. We came this far by faith, Lord. And we ask you, Father, when he get in college, Lord, to keep him, Lord, keep him protected. We thank you for him, Jesus. In Jesus's name we pray. Amen."

The family echoes, "Amen," and lets go of each other's hands. Arthur follows Coach Gray down the steps and out the front door, where he wraps his arms around his mother for one last, long good-bye. This hug is different than the silly, laughing hug at the party. Arthur knows he is really leaving, and he knows he'll miss his mother more than anyone. She knows it, too. Arthur begins to cry, and then he breaks away.

A few miles away, in Cabrini Green, William cries, too, as he hugs his mother good-bye. "I'll miss you," says Mrs. Gates.

"I'll miss you, too."

When they break apart and begin to walk toward the waiting car, Mrs. Gates gives her son one last motherly lecture. "I want you to be good, okay? Don't get mixed up in trouble. Don't get no alcohol, no wine coolers, none of that stuff."

William nods and climbs into the fancy red car, where Amaal McKaskill—another ballplayer from St. Joe's who's going to Marquette—sits in the driver's seat. William gives his mother a final hug and closes the door. Amaal starts up the engine, and they cruise out of Cabrini Green.

Mrs. Gates waves good-bye and watches the car disappear. Then she walks back slowly toward her apartment. She lingers in the doorway for a while, as if it's hard to let William go. "I just hope he stays in there," she says. "That's what worries me most. Once he gets in the door, I want him to stay in there for four years." Her voice drops lower, almost to a whisper. "I think he gonna make it. Lord, I hope so anyway."

• Epilogue •

Four years ago, all I used to dream about was playing in the NBA. I don't really dream about it like that anymore. You know, even though I love basketball, I want to do other things with my life, too. If I had to stop playing basketball right now, I think I'd still be happy. That's why when somebody say, "When you get to the NBA, don't forget about me," and all that stuff, I should say to them, "Well, if I don't make it—what, you gonna forget about me?"

—WILLIAM GATES, age 18

When I was young, when I was little, that's all I used to think about—the NBA. If I set my mind I can go. Get into a good college. I can go. But if I don't, I ain't gonna be no drug dealer, you know—cry about it, come back and stick up gas stations or nothing like that, you know. Probably go into comedy or architecture, something like that.

—ARTHUR AGEE, age 18

William started as a freshman at Marquette, but he was forced to play out of position—as a forward instead of a guard—because Kevin O'Neill had recruited too many guards. At only 6'1", William was much too small to play forward in major college basketball, and he didn't have the kind of success he had hoped for. By his sophomore year, he was coming off the bench as the sixth man. Along with his frustration about playing out of position, William was disappointed at having lost his starting job. He became Marquette's "defensive ace" and was often sent in to guard the opposing team's star player in crucial game situations.

The summer before his junior year, William married Catherine, and she and Alicia moved in with him in Milwaukee. But during the fall semester, William struggled with his academic work and grew more and more frustrated with basketball. That November, he quit the team and decided to drop out of school. But after encouragement from his family and a promise from Marquette to keep him on scholarship—even if he didn't play basketball—William stayed in school and improved his grades to a B average. After the 1993–94 season, Kevin O'Neill left Marquette and William decided to rejoin the basketball team for his senior year. The new coach has a completely different philosophy, treating his players with more consideration and allowing them to play more freely. After his season away from the game, William's knee feels stronger than ever, and he's back in his natural position as the off-guard. In an early-season double overtime win over powerful UNLV, he scored eleven points and hit two three-point shots.

For the first time in many years, William Gates loves playing basketball.

By his sophomore year, Arthur Agee had become the father of two children, Anthony and Ashley, each with a different mother. He led the Mineral Area basketball team in steals and dunks—a strange statistic for a point guard. He also led the team in jokes. Although Arthur had a successful junior college career, he displayed the same inconsistency that used to drive Luther

Bedford crazy. Coach Tim Gray commented that it seemed like there were two Arthurs and he never knew which one was going to show up for the game.

Arthur graduated from Mineral Area Junior College with a C average and received a basketball scholarship to Arkansas State University. As a junior, he was the starting point guard, and a preseason article in a national basketball magazine focused on Arthur as the key to the team's success. In his first start, he hit a thirty-foot jump shot at the buzzer to win the game.

Now a senior, Arthur Agee still dreams of playing in the NBA.